Tales from the Daytona 500

JIM HAWKINS

Sports Publishing L.L.C.
www.sportspublishingllc.com

ISBN: 1-58261-530-6

Senior acquisitions editor: Lynnette Bogard
Director of production: Susan M. Moyer
Senior project manager, book design: Jennifer L. Polson
Dust jacket designer: Joseph Brumleve
Copy editor: Cynthia L. McNew
Imaging: Kerri Baker

Printed in the United States.

Sports Publishing L.L.C.
Visit us online at www.sportspublishingllc.com

To Jack, whose motor is always running.

contents

Big Bill's Dream for America's Speed Capital

Once upon a time, which, after all, is the way all good fairy tales begin, dozens of daredevils drove their hot rods down from the hills and backwoods of Kentucky, North Carolina, Georgia and Tennessee to test their skills, man against man, on the hard-packed sands of Daytona Beach.

They came for fun. They came for pride. They came for profit. But they came. That was the important thing. They came because they simply couldn't stay away.

Many ran illegal moonshine for a living back home. Old-timers will tell you it was not unusual to walk past the jalopies waiting on the beach on race day and catch the whiff of corn whiskey in the cool sea breeze.

Compared to the impromptu midnight back-road battles, the informal jousts in farmers' corn fields, and the gritty half-mile Saturday night dirt-track duels to which most of these men were accustomed, the four-mile Daytona circuit—makeshift and at the mercy of the ebbing tides of the Atlantic Ocean—was a race car driver's dream.

Cars drive under a new pedestrian crosswalk over International Speedway Boulevard, Daytona Beach, Fla.'s main thoroughfare on Friday, Feb. 8, 2002. Several hundred thousand race fans come to Daytona Beach from early-to-mid-February for a series of motor car races that culminates with the Daytona 500. (AP Photo/Wilfredo Lee)

But race promoter William H. G. France—"Big Bill" to his friends—harbored a much bigger, much better dream. France envisioned a steeply banked oval with long straightaways where fearless drivers could hold the pedal to the metal all day long to the delight of tens of thousands of cash-carrying, speed-crazed race fans. France's vision included faster cars and bigger crowds than his fledgling, folksy sport, with its distinctive backwoods roots, had ever imagined. He foresaw an organized sport governed by a standard set of equitably applied rules and races filled with cars that were identical to those that any would-be race fan could buy and drive—not the exotic, rocket-powered machines that were idolized at the time in Indianapolis and in Europe. Today, thanks to France's foresight, determination and daring, NASCAR is America's fastest growing sport and the Daytona 500 reigns as its premier event.

It was in Daytona, Florida that NASCAR, the phenomenon that has captured the attention of the entire nation from Madison Avenue to Hollywood, was born. And Daytona remains the undisputed heart of the sport, the headquarters of NASCAR and home to what has become this country's No. 1 auto race.

The Daytona 500 is the Super Bowl of stock car racing, the highest of the so-called Redneck High Holy Days. It is an annual celebration of rebel spirit. It is a noisy, rambunctious, traditional rite of spring in a honkytonk oceanside town where, for a price, everyone is welcome to drive on the very same beach where NASCAR's fearless pioneers—brazen moonshiners and hardened men who labored in the South's textile mills—once raced.

Today, a few miles inland from that world-famous stretch of sand, souped-up hot rods annually roar inches apart around the lightning-fast, high-banked 2.5-mile oval at Daytona International Speedway at upwards of 200 mph.

When the Speedway was built in 1958, the premier race courses of the day included the relatively flat, rectangular Indianapolis Motor Speedway and the odd, egg-shaped oval at Darlington. From day one, Daytona was different. Its high banks and 2.5-mile length would quickly separate the men from the boys.

"There have been other tracks that separated the men from the boys," noted driver Jimmy Thompson, who finished

20th in the inaugural 500. "This is the track that will separate the brave from the weak, after the boys are gone."

Fast cars and Daytona Beach have been synonymous since the advent of the automotive age.

In those early days, wealthy American business tycoons with famous names like Rockefeller, Vanderbilt and Gould—names synonymous with money—regularly wintered in Daytona Beach. The town was founded by Mathias Day, who had migrated south from Ohio in 1870. The cooler climate in Daytona was considered more hospitable than tropical South Florida.

But the area's main attraction was the remarkably wide beach, which stretched uninterrupted from Ormond, north of Daytona, to Ponce Inlet, south of town.

Bicycles, horse-drawn buggies, and finally, motorized carriages all found the smooth, hard-packed sand accommodating. Daytona soon became synonymous with speed. Before there was an Indianapolis 500 (1911), before there was a 24-hour race at Le Mans (1923), bold men were racing new-fangled contraptions known as automobiles on the hard-packed sands of Daytona Beach.

In the early years of the 20th century, automotive pioneers Ransom E. Olds and Alexander Winton journeyed to Florida in pursuit of speed and the opportunity to demonstrate the abilities of their fascinating new machines. Imaginative hotel owners saw Daytona's early Winter Speed Carnivals (1903-1910), forerunners of today's incredibly popular Speed Weeks, as a way to fill rooms with vacationers eager to escape the cold and snow up north. With the surf on one side and sand dunes on the other and no barriers in sight, Daytona's unusually wide beach seemed like the perfect place to determine just how fast these new motorized vehicles could be made to go.

In March of 1903, Ransom Olds, who would later attch his family name to the Oldsmobile, became the first man to stage a timed run on the sand. After he was clocked at the then awesome speed of 50 mph while racing his "Pirate" on Ormond Beach, just north of Daytona, Olds enthusiastically declared, "You have no idea what a thrill it is out there." Nine months later, Orville and Wilbur Wright took to the air for the first time at Kitty Hawk, North Carolina.

It was in 1904, however, that the automobile really put Daytona Beach on the speed map. On the ice of frozen Lake St. Clair, north of Detroit, Barney Oldfield, piloting Henry Ford's "999" racer, set a world land speed record by averaging 91.37 mph. Duly challenged, two weeks later, William Kissam Vanderbilt Jr., driving a Mercedes imported from Germany, began Daytona's second Winter Speed Carnival by erasing Oldfield's mark with a 92.308 mph clocking of his own.

In all, 11 world records and four U.S. records were shattered by the various classes of cars competing at Daytona in 1904. A 1905 movie, *Automotive Races at Ormond, Florida,* further enhanced the image and reputation of Daytona Beach.

Racing on Daytona Beach in 1905, wealthy New York sportsman Frank Croker swerved his car sharply into the ocean waves at high speed to avoid a motorcyclist who had inadvertently ventured out into his path. Croker and his riding mechanic were both killed—the first racing fatalities at Daytona Beach. Recognizing that their obsession with speed was quickly becoming too dangerous for amateurs, auto developers began hiring professional drivers such as cigar-chomping showman

Barney Oldfield and Switzerland's Louis Chevrolet, who later would lend his family name to General Motors.

European racing rivals Major Henry Segrave and Sir Malcolm Campbell also left their marks on Daytona Beach. During the late 1920s and '30s, the world's land speed record was shattered on the beach with remarkable regularity. Segrave, piloting a squat 1,000-horsepower vehicle propelled by two V-12 airplane engines, reached 203.97 mph on a measured mile on the hard-packed sand in 1927, the same year baseball's Babe Ruth belted his milestone 60 home runs. It was the first time any driver had ever exceeded 200 mph anywhere. Incredibly, it was also the first time Segrave had ever laid eyes on Daytona Beach.

When he returned in 1929, Segrave, the first driver to wear a crash helmet, was clocked at 231 mph. After Segrave was killed in England trying to improve upon his own world water speed record, Sir Malcolm Campbell, driving his long, sleek Bluebird, was clocked at 330 mph on Daytona Beach and made an honorary citizen of the city.

Nevertheless, record seekers soon relocated their pursuits to the smoother, wider Bonneville Salt Flats of Utah, unwittingly leaving Daytona Beach to the race car drivers. One of the spectators who had watched with great interest as Campbell sped across the sand at 330 mph in 1935 was a 26-year-old mechanic named Bill France.

Harry Truman was residing in the White House. Jackie Robinson would soon shatter baseball's color barrier. Ronald Reagan had recently been elected president—of the Screen Actors Guild. And many people thought Bill France had sand in his eyes in December of 1947 when he laid out his plan to transform the wild and woolly backwoods sport of stock car racing into a neatly unified organization that would compete on Daytona Beach and elsewhere throughout the South.

The Great Depression had driven France, his wife Anne, and their infant son Billy out of Washington D.C. in the fall of 1934. Towing a small house trailer behind their Hupmobile, France and his family headed south along the highway toward Miami. As they approached the city of Daytona, already famed for the world speed records that had been set on its trademark beach, Bill—a mechanic by trade but a racer at heart—made a spontaneous left turn and headed for the nearby ocean.

And the history of motor sports in America was forever altered.

France, whose lifelong love affair with racing began when he secretly raced his father's Model T on small tracks in the Baltimore/Washington area, chafed at the dishonesty of many race organizers in those early years and at the fact that at its most successful upper levels, auto racing remained primarily a rich man's sport. France dreamed of someday rectifying both situations. The visionary France was convinced American race fans would love to watch race cars that closely resembled the cars they themselves drove at home.

Stock car drivers first raced one another on Daytona Beach on March 8, 1936. Civic leaders and businessmen, eager to maintain Daytona's image as America's automotive speed capital after the world record setters departed, put up a $5,000 purse, which was sufficient to lure many of the best race car drivers in the nation, including 1934 Indianapolis 500 champion "Wild Bill" Cummings, to the beach.

The first stock race on Daytona Beach, scheduled for 250 miles, was a disaster. Cars became mired in the rutted sand on the 3.2-mile course that encompassed both the beach and the adjacent paved public roadway, and the race had to be halted early. The city reportedly lost $22,000 on the venture. Driving a 1935 Ford with a V-8 engine, now local mechanic Bill France finished fifth.

In 1938, after many of Daytona Beach's most influential citizens had soured on the financial merits of auto racing, France joined forces with a local restaurant owner to promote a couple of races himself. The two partners made a $200 profit on their first race, then doubled the price of admission to a dollar and pocketed $2,200 on the second race later that summer.

Bill France was convinced he was on the right path.

The National Association for Stock Car Automobile Racing—NASCAR for short—was born on December 14, 1947, when two dozen drivers, mechanics and racing entrepreneurs gathered in the smoky Roof Garden bar at the Streamline Hotel in Daytona Beach. Over whiskey, France explained his concept of a racing series that featured everyday men driving everyday cars and acing at prices everyone could afford.

"We don't know how big stock car racing can be," France admitted. "But I do know that if stock car racing is handled properly, it can go the way big car [Indy car] racing has gone."

France laid out the rules: All cars would have to be clean, undented—at least when the races began—brightly painted, and strictly stock. The rules would be uniform and fairly enforced. And, maybe most important of all, the new organization would be ruled by one man: Six-foot-five, 220-pound Bill France.

NASCAR's original official rules were printed on a single sheet of paper. Cars had to include complete bodies, fenders and hood. For safety's sake, headlights had to be removed or covered with masking tape, mufflers and rear seat cushions had to be removed, the front seat had to be intact, and the doors had to be strapped shut to keep them from flying open on contact during the race. There are no doors on today's race cars. Drivers climb in and out through the left front window.

The first NASCAR race was run at Daytona Beach on Feb. 15, 1948—six days before the organization was officially incorporated. Since no new cars had been produced in this country during World War II, the field was filled with "late model" vehicles, many of which had been modified. Fifty-six drivers from a dozen different states showed up for the 68-lap race on the new 2.2-mile course that again included both the wide, hard-packed beach and the adjacent, bumpy, narrow, two-lane blacktop of highway A1A. In an effort to cool their brakes, so vital when it came time to execute the sharp turns at each end of the makeshift track, drivers often raced on the edge of the water.

The crowd, estimated at 14,000, paid $2.50 apiece to sit atop their cars or stand in the sand alongside the track, which was often delineated by nothing more than a rope and lined with fuel trucks, as the colorfully painted cars roared past.

The winner was World War II veteran Red Byron, a bomber tail gunner whose left leg had been badly mangled when his plane was shot down.

Even then, NASCAR displayed a knack for delivering the best possible story.

To discourage gate crashers, Bill France Sr. posted signs that warned "Beware of Rattlesnakes" at various vantage points along the beach. At dawn on race day, France walked up and down the beach, waking up fans and tourists and revelers who had spent the night imbibing and sleeping on the sand. France gave them two options: they could pay $2.50 and stick around to watch the race—or they could leave the premises.

In those early years, the drivers often slept in their cars, too. "If you needed a new tire [for your race car], that meant you had to give up your hotel room," recalled Frank Mundy, who was present when NASCAR was formed and won three early races. "You couldn't afford to pay for both."

The beach races quickly proved so popular that they often attracted as many as 20,000 race fans and curious gawkers. France's son Billy, who would later succeed his father as president of NASCAR, often sold snow cones to the crowd.

Today's wildly successful Winston Cup Series was initially known as the Strictly Stock Division when it debuted in Charlotte, N.C. on June 19, 1949. But the fields for the early races on Daytona Beach featured various classes—Modified, Convertible, and Grand National—and were sometimes filled with as many as 124 cars.

The more the merrier, as far as the seagulls were concerned. To them, the cars made inviting targets.

"Every one of them thought we were driving a Porta-John," early beach racer Tim Flock recalled.

The early primitive beach races lacked the organization and amenities that drivers and race fans today take for granted in NASCAR.

"They would qualify us in straight-line speed," recalled pioneer driver Ned Jarrett, whose son Dale would later win the 500 three times. "You'd go down the beach for a mile to get your speed up, then they'd clock you for a mile."

Ned Jarrett recalled one such beach race in the early 1950s.

"We got up in the morning of the race and it was a little misty," Jarrett explained. "It wasn't raining, just a heavy fog. The sand was wet. You couldn't see very far in front of you because of the fog."

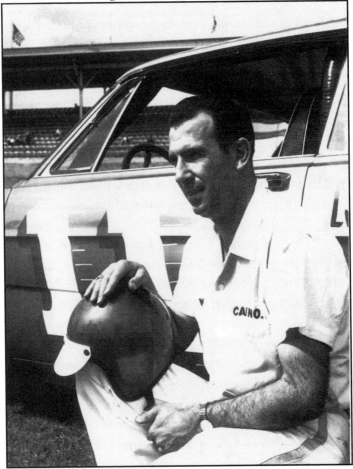

Race car driver Ned Jarrett, 32, of Camden, N.J. is shown in 1965. (AP Photo)

In fact, the drivers could barely see beyond the fronts of their hoods. Today, no race would be allowed to begin under such conditions.

"When I went on the beach part of the course, the cars ahead of me were throwing up water and sand," Jarrett continued. "I was cruising up the beach at 100 mph, and all of a sudden I got hit in the back by one of those modified cars running 30 or 40 mph faster than I was.

"My car turned sideways, dug into the sand, and started rolling. I wound up in the ocean. I got knocked out momentarily. One of the track attendants came over to help me."

Meanwhile, with Jarrett's jalopy in the water and therefore safely out of the way, the race roared on.

Disoriented from the impact, with blood streaming down his face from the gash in his head, Jarrett broke free from the fellow who had come to his assistance and stumbled through traffic back across the beach.

"There were cars coming up through there and only through the grace of God did I get across there," Jarrett recalled. "They had a string that separated the course from the spectators. I got to that string and passed out. Or so I was told."

After several minutes, Jarrett awoke in a spectator's arms.

"I was in some fat lady's arms and she had about a third of a pint of Early Times whiskey, trying to get me to drink it," Jarrett said. "I was pretty sure I was going to die because I had cut my head and blood was coming down across my face. I was hurtin' all over. I didn't want no whiskey because I figured that would kill my chances of getting through the pearly gates."

NASCAR had only one ambulance available that afternoon, so Bill France asked a Florida highway patrolman to drive Ned Jarrett to the nearest hospital.

"I was just beat up," Jarrett recalled. "They needed the ambulance in case somebody got really hurt."

In the early years, NASCAR was often at odds with the powerful American Automobile Association, which sanctioned the prestigious Indianapolis 500 and was considered the premier racing body in this country. So deep was AAA's resentment of NASCAR that when Bill France was spotted in the garage area prior to the 1954 Indy 500, AAA officials had the NASCAR founder ushered out of famed Gasoline Alley.

France went home and eventually built his own track and established a 500-mile race that would soon surpass even Indy.

In 1955, Bill France and NASCAR withstood an effort in the United States Senate to ban auto racing in this country after two-time Indianapolis 500 champion Billy Vukovich and Formula One champion Alberto Ascari had been killed in racing accidents and Pierre Levegh's Mercedes crashed into the grandstand at the 24 Hours of Le Mans, killing not only the driver but more than 80 spectators on the spot. Some 50 others who were injured in Levegh's crash died later.

No politician would dare propose such a ban today, given NASCAR's incredible widespread popularity. But in 1955, stock car racing was generally dismissed as a southern anomaly, and France had little clout outside of his own sport.

It was the surge in popularity of Daytona's beach races in the early 1950s that also doomed them. As the city of Daytona Beach grew, and attendance at the stock car races increased, the need for a permanent race track with ample seating and parking became apparent. Those early beach races caused massive traffic jams—not that today's races at Daytona International Speedway don't. Citizens and tourists alike complained about the noise and the crowds, which together made more traditional beach activities, such as relaxation, swimming and sun-bathing, impossible. Along Highway A1A, which served as the paved backstretch of Daytona's makeshift race course, cars often reached speeds of 150 mph. When more and more people began building homes along A1A, right on the race course, France realized the days of stock car racing on Daytona Beach were numbered.

And, of course, on the beach, drivers, spectators and race organizers alike always had to contend with the incoming tide. Not even Big Bill France could control that. In 1952, the start of Daytona's Grand National stock car race had to be delayed for nearly an hour while fans maneuvered their family vehicles into viewing position along the beach course. To beat the incoming high tide, the race was reduced from 48 to 37 laps. Even so, some spectators' cars became partially submerged before they could get off the beach.

France first proposed building a new state-of-the-art superspeedway in Daytona in 1953. As early as 1954, France was optimistically advertising that year's event as the "Last Race on the Beach."

But it wasn't to be that easy.

One would-be builder, Lou Perini, who had pledged $3 million to the project, backed out at the last minute when his engineers warned him the two-lane highways leading in and out of Daytona couldn't possibly handle all the traffic that the proposed new speedway would attract. After years of civic wrangling and political debate, France finally announced that he would build his dream track himself for the bargain basement price of $750,000 on swamp land adjacent to the city airport at the west end of town.

To secure the dirt needed to build up Daytona International Speedway's high banks, which enable drivers to circle the 2.5-mile oval with their gas pedals pushed hard to the floor the whole way, a 44-acre lake was dug in the middle of what would eventually become the infield. In all, more than a million cubic yards of earth had to be moved during construction.

"People just couldn't believe its size," Bill France Jr. recalled. "They said things like, 'Who's going to race on it?'"

During the latter stages of the construction of the 2.5-mile paved oval, many wondered how slow a car could travel around the steep turns without rolling downhill into the grass. The banking at Daytona International Speedway is 31 degrees. That was as steep as construction workers could stack the dirt and the lime rock that lies beneath the asphalt without having it all slide back down to the bottom.

One of France's earliest supporters in the construction of Daytona International Speedway was the Pure Oil Company. Pure Oil and 76 Fuel contributed cash and a $35,000 line of credit for the fuel that was needed for the construction equipment in exchange for a contract as "the official fuel provider." Union 76 is still the official fuel of Daytona International Speedway and NASCAR.

At one point during construction, Bill France found himself in dire need of an immediate $30,000. He called an executive he knew at Coca-Cola and offered to advertise Coke in every program at every NASCAR race for the next 10 years and to make Coke the official soft drink at Daytona International Speedway—if only the company would kick in the needed $30,000. Coke declined, and France called rival Pepsi, which promptly ponied up the cash. Concessionaires have been pouring Pepsi at Daytona ever since.

The last NASCAR race on the beach was held in 1958, on a gray, chilly day before a crowd of 35,000. A few miles inland, a high-banked 2.5-mile paved oval was already under construction.

Bill France, who had borrowed $600,000 to build the initial 18,000-seat grandstand, immediately began selling tickets to the 1959 race. He then turned around and used that ticket money to build additional seating at the track.

Race cars drivers and race fans alike had never seen anything remotely resembling sprawling Daytona International Speedway when it debuted on Feb. 22, 1959. Drivers quickly discovered there was no need or reason to tap their brakes. In fact, to do so often spelled defeat. The bumping and banging so commonplace on the half-mile dirt tracks to which most of the drivers were accustomed became highly dangerous at the high speeds of Daytona.

"We were all a bunch of rookies going 30 to 40 miles an hour faster than we ever had before in our lives," admitted stock car racing pioneer and family patriarch Lee Petty, winner of the inaugural 500 in 1959. "There were some scared cats out there."

Richard Petty's younger brother Maurice, who was also a driver but became better known for his skills as a mechanic, arrived at the new track with his father and brother for the first Daytona 500 in 1959.

"I thought, 'There ain't no way they're going to be able to race on this race track,'" Maurice later recalled. "It was too big. It was ungodly big. It was something none of us had ever seen, or dreamed of seeing. It was a whole new ballgame."

Moonshine is out. Milk is in. Nobody in NASCAR runs moonshine any more. They are too busy making money other ways. Tons of money.

The changing face of NASCAR in the 21st century is reflected both in the drivers and in the fans in the grandstands at Daytona.

"It's not the same core NASCAR people," admitted Kevin Harvick, who roared to stardom in 2001, winning two Winston Cup races, Rookie of the Year honors, and the Busch Series championship as well. Harvick was hired by Richard Childress Racing to replace stock car racing icon Dale Earnhardt, who was killed in a 2001 crash at Daytona. "It's people who like to wear their hats backwards and like to watch MTV," Harvick noted. "Those are things I like to do."

The intricate machines that make up the show on the open-wheel circuits of the Indy Racing League, Championship Auto Racing Teams, and European favorite Formula One are sleek, swift and high-tech. At Daytona, men (and occasionally a woman, too) drive candy-colored Chevys, Fords, Dodges and Pontiacs—cars that everyday people are familiar with, cars they can relate to, cars that look just like the ones they themselves drive at home every day.

In the mid-1980s, stock car racing king Richard Petty estimated the size of NASCAR's hard-core audience at two million fans. But a poll commissioned by NASCAR in 2001 calculated the number of "core fans"—people who have "a real passion for NASCAR"—at 41 million. According to the study, if you add in the curious newcomers and casual observers who are increasingly attracted to the sport, that number grows to 75 million. Which explains why in 2001, NASCAR was able to sign an eye-popping six-year, $2.4 billion national TV bonanza with NBC, Fox and TBS.

Each February more than 175,000 devoted fans make the pilgrimage to the motor sports Mecca that is Daytona

Beach. Unlike Indianapolis—where relatively few fans bother to show up any more except on the actual day of open-wheel racing's own world-famous 500—stock car aficionados faithfully flock to Daytona for a week or more each spring. By Friday night during race week every motel for miles around is flashing its "No Vacancy" sign. Even seedy, shopworn rooms that normally sell for $35 or less rent for $150 or more a night during Speed Weeks.

When the unmuffled motors of the stock cars spring to life, you can almost feel the ground shake. The Daytona 500 is truly a religious experience.

The elite, the affluent and the lucky attending the Daytona 500 stay in oceanfront hotels or in their lushly carpeted, state-of-the-art motor homes and RVs, complete with microwave ovens and satellite dishes, that annually form a small city at the west end of the track's massive infield. By race day the runways of the adjacent airport, just beyond the backstretch of Daytona International Speedway, are lined with private and corporate jets, monuments to the new-found popularity and affluence of the stock car sport.

Inside the Daytona Club, thousands of well-heeled patrons can watch the big race while feasting on prime rib, made-to-order crepes, and $100-a-bottle wine, all served by bow-tied waiters. Even the portable toilets in the Daytona Club are wood-paneled, with framed artwork on the walls and gold-accented fixtures—a far cry from the facilities folks frequent in the infield. Another 5,000 fans can relax in the 66 luxury suites at Daytona International Speedway, which rent for $40,000 to $150,000 a year.

Attending the Daytona 500 is no longer a day at the beach.

At the east end of the Speedway's infield, where the songs of Waylon Jennings and Jerry Lee Lewis are everyday anthems, folks sleep in tents or beneath their barely running retired school buses. No shirts, no shoes, no showers are required here. Occasionally, revelers do bathe with garden hoses. Sunburns are inevitable. Bibbed overalls and deodorant are optional. Debauchery rules. Fans grill sausage, chicken and steak while others munch on lunch meat. It is always happy hour. Beer consumption is measured by the case, not by the bottle or can.

It has been estimated that if all of the hot dogs annually sold at Daytona International Speedway during Speed Weeks were placed end to end, the wieners would circle the 2.5-mile asphalt oval three times.

Here and there, a Confederate flag can be seen flapping in the breeze, a throwback to stock car racing's redneck roots. But as Tennessee-born, two-time Daytona 500 champ Sterling Marlin likes to say, "There ain't many of us [rednecks] left."

That was Bill France Sr.'s legacy—a legacy that lives and thrives to this day, beyond even Big Bill's wildest dreams. It is safe to say that no individual has ever played a greater role in creating, shaping and nurturing any other sport. And it is common knowledge that France ruled that sport with an iron hand. When bearded Fidel Castro forced President Fulgencio Batista to flee Cuba in 1959, Batista temporarily took up residence in Daytona Beach. That inspired *Charlotte News* sportswriter Max Muhlmann to write, "Now there are two dictators in Daytona Beach, Fulgencio Batista and Bill France." France was furious. He immediately flew to Charlotte in an unsuccessful effort to get Muhlmann fired.

Today, a statue of Bill France Sr. stands at Daytona International Speedway. But Big Bill does not stand alone. Appropriately, Anne, France's wife of nearly six decades, stands beside him, Bill's arm around her waist.

"While Dad was climbing high to reach his far-out goals, Mom held the ladder," their son and future NASCAR president Bill France Jr. later explained. "Dad had vision and dreams. Mom was his reality."

For years, before the Daytona 500 simply grew too large, Anne Bledsoe France sold the tickets, counted the money and kept the books. Bill France Sr., by then 62, stepped aside in 1972 and turned the day-to-day management of Daytona International Speedway and NASCAR over to his son, Bill Jr.

Bill Sr. and Anne France both passed away in 1992, two months apart, partners to the end.

The First 500

Bill France, who had poured his heart and soul—as well as all of the money he could muster—into the construction of Daytona International Speedway, could not have orchestrated a more exciting, newsworthy finish to the inaugural Daytona 500 if he had tried. To this day, the 1959 Daytona 500 ranks as one of the most memorable motor sports finishes of all time as Lee Petty, Johnny Beauchamp and Joe Weatherly crossed the finish line three abreast, side by side.

As the cars roared out of turn four for the 200th and final time, Beauchamp, a relative unknown from Iowa, elected to go low on the track. When Weatherly—two laps behind the leaders but nevertheless racing along with them—went high, Petty, the stock car racing pioneer and reigning Grand National champion who had swapped the lead with Beauchamp a dozen times during the final 49 laps, found himself in the middle of the track. As the three cars streaked across the finish line, the fact that Weatherly was on the outside, closest to the

Johnny Beauchamp (73), driving a 1959 Thunderbird and Lee Petty, (42), driving an Oldsmobile were neck and neck on the last lap of the 500-mile late stock car and convertible race over the Daytona International Speedway February 22, 1959, but Petty nosed out Beauchamp at the finish line. The average speed for the race was 135.521 miles per hour. (AP Photo)

flag stand and to the crowd, made it difficult for the naked eye to pick out the winner.

Bill France Sr. and flagman Johnny Brunner both thought Beauchamp in his Ford Thunderbird had been the first across the finish line. Upstairs, in the control tower, Bill France Jr. wasn't so sure. A dozen writers polled in the press box all picked Petty, who obviously agreed and immediately proceeded to Victory Lane, where he informed all who would listen that he had won the race. When the public address announcer proclaimed Beauchamp the winner, many skeptical, eagle-eyed spectators booed.

Beauchamp, who had been all alone with Petty on the lead lap for the final 125 miles, insisted he had finished in front by about 18 inches. Heralded as the unofficial winner,

Beauchamp was presented with the winner's trophy. But Petty remained unconvinced.

The photo of the finish, hastily snapped and then hurriedly developed by the track photographer, clearly showed Weatherly's lapped car in front, followed by Petty—with Beauchamp about three feet behind Lee, his front bumper even with the back edge of Petty's hood. However, all three cars were still several feet short of the finish line when the track photographer, who was stationed a couple of feet beyond the finish line, had snapped the critical picture. As a result, track officials elected to wait until newsreel footage of the finish could be found and examined three days later, 61 hours after the actual conclusion of the race—and after the dispute had kept the inaugural Daytona 500 in the headlines of the nation's sports sections for three additional days.

Four days after the checkered flag waved above the finish line, Lee Petty—who had stuck around Daytona, convinced that he would eventually be vindicated and declared the winner—was handed the trophy and the $19,050 first-place check.

"Man, I'd never have believed it myself that there could be a 500-mile race like this one," said a relieved Petty. "It was close. Too close. But I knew I won it. Because I was there."

Ironically, the racing careers of both Lee Petty and Johnny Beauchamp effectively ended when the two collided trying to avoid a spinning car on the track ahead of them and crashed at Daytona on the last lap of the second qualifying race for the 1961 500.

In the first qualifying heat, Petty had watched his son Richard walk away from a serious crash when the younger Petty's Plymouth flew over the guard rail and into the parking lot below. Richard's car was demolished, and doctors later discovered dozens of tiny slivers of broken glass in both of his eyes.

On the final lap of the second qualifying race, Lee Petty and Beauchamp collided. Like his son had done earlier, Petty flew over the guard rail and off of the track. When Lee's car finally came to rest 100 feet away in a parking lot, he had sustained a punctured lung, multiple internal injuries and several broken bones. Beauchamp, whose car tore through the fence and over the embankment along with Petty's, suffered serious head injuries in the crash and never raced NASCAR again.

From his hospital bed, the gravely injured elder Petty turned to NASCAR president Bill France and joked, "Bill, I want you to take Richard's driver's license away from him and get him a pilot's license." When France pointed out that Lee Petty's vehicle had actually traveled farther through the air than his son's did, Lee replied, "Well, then, maybe you'd better get me a pilot's license, too."

There were only about 6,000 hotel rooms in the Daytona Beach area in 1959. Then, as now, they were virtually all filled on the weekend of the first 500.

The first Daytona 500 attracted 59 cars and 41,921 paying customers. But according to newspaper reports, the crowd was actually larger than that. Hundreds of fans were seen crawling under the fence to get into the track, even though admission to the infield was only $4.

Bill France, who had poured every penny he could beg or borrow into building the Speedway, reportedly grossed $500,000 from the race—money he desperately needed to begin paying his bills.

The very first race over the new asphalt oval—two days before the inaugural Daytona 500—featured convertibles and covered 100 miles, 40 laps around the track. The convertible chase was conducted in conjunction with an identical 100-mile qualifying race for NASCAR Grand National racers later the same day. That established a tradition that continues at Daytona to this day—the annual Twin 125 qualifying races on the Thursday before the big race.

The inaugural Daytona 500 was a so-called "sweepstakes" event that included cars from both NASCAR's Grand National and Convertible divisions. However, drivers of the convertibles quickly discovered they were operating at a distinct aerodynamic disadvantage against the hardtops at the high speeds made possible by Daytona's long straightaways and steep banking. Not surprisingly, 1959 was the only year in which convertibles competed in the Daytona 500.

When Daytona International Speedway opened the track for its first time trials in February 1959, NASCAR president Bill France was one of the first to take a test lap around the 2.5-mile oval. Although he had retired as an active driver years earlier, France, piloting a '59 Pontiac Catalina, posted a lap of 114 mph.

The fastest lap any driver had turned in anywhere on the NASCAR circuit during the 1958 season had been a mere 116.952 mph by Eddie Pagan during pole qualifying for the Southern 500 at Darlington Raceway. The world record for a closed course at the time was 177.038 mph—a mark that had been set by Tony Bettenhausen Sr. at Monza, Italy, the previous June.

Bill France Sr. may have had the famed Indianapolis Motor Speedway in the back of his mind when he built his new race track. But the high banks of Daytona soon proved to be no place for open-wheel Indy cars. In an effort to demonstrate that his new oval was the fastest track in the world, Bill France invited several Indy car teams to test at Daytona. Daytona hometown hero Marshall Teague, who had excelled in the earlier beach course races, was killed in February 1959 in a spectacular crash during an exhibition run on the new track. In April of 1959, pole winner George Amick was killed in the first and only Indy car race ever run at Daytona. However, no NASCAR driver died in the Daytona 500 until Dale Earnhardt in 2001. The inaugural Daytona 500 was accident-free. There was not a single yellow caution flag during the entire race.

Although he won the race, Lee Petty admitted to being initially intimidated by Daytona International Speedway.

"This track was really different, so big it made you wonder about things," Petty admitted afterwards. "I'll tell you what: there wasn't a man there who wasn't scared to death of the place. What it amounted to was that we were all a bunch of rookies, going 30 to 40 miles an hour faster than we ever had before in our lives."

3

The King

There have been drivers who were blessed with faster cars. There have been drivers who were born with more raw nerve. But in NASCAR, there has only been one King.

Richard Petty won a record 200 NASCAR races, including seven Daytona 500s. In 1967, in a performance that most certainly will never be equaled, he won 27 times, including ten races in a row. He won seven Winston Cup championships, and for eighteen consecutive seasons (1960-77), he visited Victory Lane at least once.

To Richard Petty, driving race cars was an art—one he practiced with dominating efficiency at Daytona.

Richard Petty later recalled the first time he laid eyes on massive Daytona International Speedway as he arrived with his father, Lee, and brother, Maurice, for the inaugural 500.

"We came out of the tunnel under the fourth turn, into

the infield, and suddenly it was like being on the surface of the moon," Petty remembered. "It was mostly barren, still a construction site. And way in the distance, you could see that high banking of the first and second turns. It looked like it must have been 30 miles down there to the banking."

Richard Petty raced a used '57 Oldsmobile convertible in the inaugural Daytona 500 in 1959, a race that was won by his dad. Richard, who was 21 years old at the time, blew an engine and completed just eight of the 200 laps. He finished 57th in the 59-car field.

Two days earlier, young Petty had gotten his first taste of the new speedway when he participated in the preliminary convertible race. Richard was immediately impressed by the length of the new oval. "I thought I would never get back around," he admitted.

The 1959 Daytona 500 marked the first time Petty's car carried the number 43. The young Petty, who had participated in eight NASCAR Grand National events in 1958, had previously raced as car number 2. "I came along at the right time for Daytona and Daytona came along at the right time for me," he would reminisce later. "We grew up together."

Along with many of his veteran rivals, Richard Petty discovered that Daytona's high speeds made it possible to duck in under the "draft" of the car just ahead of him on the track, using that car to break the wind and allow him to ease off the throttle a bit in his own vehicle without losing any speed. Petty also discovered that when he wanted to make a move, he could step on the gas and "slingshot" past the car ahead. "It was almost like finding extra horsepower," Richard explained.

Petty finished a distant second, 27 seconds behind Fireball Roberts, at Daytona in 1962. It was an indication of bigger and better days to come.

"That boy, Richard Petty, did a wonderful job of driving," Roberts raved. "He just drove the hell out of that car."

"I was just waiting for [Roberts] to blow up," a grinning Petty admitted.

Backed by a powerful 436-cubic-inch "Hemi" engine in his Plymouth, Richard Petty grabbed the lead on the 52nd lap of the 1964 Daytona 500 and never looked back en route to his first superspeedway win.

"The feeling of the Hemi was unbelievable," Petty later recalled in his biography. "The power was there all the time. It didn't matter when you punched it; it socked you right back in your seat. It sounded like it was going to suck the hood in."

The Hemi, so named because of its distinctive hemispherical combustion chamber, had first been installed in the Kiekhaefer Chrysler 300s on the Grand National circuit in the 1950s. Following accidents that claimed the lives of Fireball Roberts and Joe Weatherly, the Chrysler Hemi engines and the high-rise cylinder heads that Ford wanted to introduce were banned from NASCAR in 1965 in an effort to slow the cars down and increase safety. As a result, Chrysler and many of its drivers withdrew from NASCAR at the start of the 1965 season. The Dodges and Plymouths returned midway through the year when NASCAR relaxed its ban and allowed the Hemi engines back with certain restrictions. Ultimately, the Hemi proved too powerful for passenger cars, and production was discontinued by Chrysler.

In 1966, Petty became the first driver to win the 500 more than once. Despite seven pit stops, Petty averaged a record 160.27 mph and was comfortably running a full lap in front of his closest competitor, Cale Yarborough, when rain halted the race two laps short of the full 500 miles.

Petty's third Daytona triumph came in 1971, when Richard's Plymouth Road Runner was one of only two factory-backed entries in the first Daytona 500 to be run with restrictor plates. That signaled the start of one of King Richard's greatest seasons—a year in which he won 21 races and his third Grand National driving championship.

From 1971 through 1974, the dominating Petty won three out of four Daytona 500s, interrupted only by A. J. Foyt in 1972, and three out of four Winston Cup championships.

At the 1973 Daytona 500, Petty won for the fourth time when Buddy Baker, who was closing in with six laps to go, suddenly blew an engine. In fact, Petty probably won the race on their final pit stop, when Richard was in and out of his pit in eight seconds, gambling by sticking with worn tires, while Baker made a 10-second stop. Buddy was trying to make up that difference when his car quit.

"I can't believe it, I just can't believe it," Baker said later. "I had it won. I haven't gotten over the shock. I still think I'm leading the race."

The record book credits Petty with running 200 laps to win his second Daytona 500 in a row—and the fifth of his incredible run—in 1974. In reality, the first 20 laps never happened, as Bill France scaled back the 500 to 450 miles in response to the oil crisis that gripped the country. The 1974 Daytona 500 actually began on the 21st lap. Otherwise, it was racing as usual as King Richard again ended up in Victory Lane.

"This is a hard race, and you have to be both good and lucky to win 'er," Petty said. "We've been both, which is the only way I can explain why we've won five and no one else has won more than one."

Petty arrived in Daytona in February 1979 just two months after undergoing major stomach surgery. Few expected him to seriously contend, much less win the race. Certainly he did not have the strongest car. That distinction belonged to pole sitter Buddy Baker. Besides, Petty was immersed in the longest drought of his brilliant career. He had not won a race anywhere in more than a year, 45 starts earlier.

But what really made Petty's sixth Daytona 500 win special was the fact that earlier in the week's activities, Richard's 18-year-old son Kyle, who was making his racing debut in the ARCA series, had also finished first. Afterwards, Lee Petty, Richard and Kyle—three generations of successful racers—all celebrated together in Victory Lane.

Richard's seventh Daytona victory was hard-won, in part due to new NASCAR restrictions on race cars. With the country confronted by an energy crisis, NASCAR downsized its cars in 1981, mandating that the wheelbases be shortened from 115 inches to 110. The result was boxy-looking vehicles, with steeply sloped rear windows, that were difficult to handle.

"It scares me tee-totally, absolutely to death," declared the always colorful Darrell Waltrip, who likened the Daytona experience that year to driving down a busy freeway at 70 mph with four flat tires.

Despite the drivers' concerns over the safety of the newly downsized cars—or perhaps because of them—the race was relatively accident-free, with only four caution flags for minor incidents.

With 24 laps to go, the legendary Petty gambled and took only gas on his final pit stop, not wanting to wait around for new tires. Petty's brief 6.8-second stop catapulted him into the lead, and he hung on to win his seventh and final Daytona

500, edging Bobby Allison, who had run out of gas on the 174th lap and had been forced to coast into the pits.

"We've won 500s where we out-ran 'em, where we out-lucked 'em, where we out-everythinged 'em," the mustachioed Petty proclaimed. "Now you can add a new one. We out-thunk 'em."

In Victory Lane after the race, Richard Petty proudly hoisted his seven-month-old grandson Adam, who was sucking on his pacifier, into the air. Nineteen years later, promising young Adam Petty—the first fourth-generation racer in major motor sports history and heir to one of the most famous names in auto racing—was tragically killed on a Mother's Day weekend crash in New Hampshire while practicing for a Busch race.

Petty won the Daytona 500 in 1964, 1966, and 1971 driving Plymouths. He was behind the wheel of a Dodge Charger when he finished first in 1973 and '74. He won with an Olds Cutlass in 1979 and a Buick in 1981.

Richard led his first laps in the Daytona 500—29 of them—in 1960 after Tommy Herbert was involved in a crash that sent the engine flying out of his car.

In 1973, Petty posted the widest margin of victory in Daytona 500 history when he finished more than two laps ahead of runner-up Bobby Isaac.

Petty's ulcers were acting up in 1976, and he spent the week swigging Maalox straight out of the bottle while he was in the garage and even in the pits. But there was no way The King would ever willingly miss a race.

Unlike his demanding, no-nonsense father Lee, Richard Petty proved himself to be a charmer. Prior to his 1964 victory at Daytona, Petty had enjoyed his greatest successes on

NASCAR's short tracks. That was where his first 28 victories all occurred. By then the ever-friendly, always smiling Petty had become the sport's most popular pilot. He was never too busy or too preoccupied to autograph a fan's program, even though it took him nearly 10 seconds to affix his elaborate signature.

A 1992 Petty autograph session drew 65,000 people. And that fancy autograph was no accident. Early in his career, Petty enrolled in a handwriting course at Kings Business College in Greensboro, N.C. to perfect that art.

Following a wreck in the 1988 Daytona 500, Richard Petty, who surprisingly had suffered nothing more serious than a sprained ankle, was lying on a stretcher in the infield care center when his worried wife reached his side. Lynda Petty had been pleading with her husband to retire, repeatedly suggesting that it was time to quit. But Petty had insisted he wasn't going to retire as long as he was still having fun racing.

"Well," Lynda Petty inquired, with tears in her eyes as her husband lay on a stretcher, "are we still having fun?"

The Intimidator

Dale Earnhardt was, at one and the same time, beloved and despised. Widely revered, he was also ridiculed for his early recklessness. He was resented by many for his aggressive, go-for-broke style and the fact that he became rich beyond almost anyone's wildest dreams.

He was fearless. He was "The Intimidator." He was stubborn. He was "Ironhead." He was the "Man in Black," the most popular driver since The King, Richard Petty. He was the last of stock car racing's dirt-track daredevils to strike it rich.

Cocky behind the wheel of his race car, hardened by years under the lights on the short tracks, but publicly shy because of his lack of formal education and his cotton milltown upbringing, Earnhardt gradually grew into his role as a multimillionaire businessman and the premier spokesman for his sport.

Driver Dale Earnhardt, center, team owner Richard Childress, left, and Bobby Hutchens pose in Victory Lane after Earnhardt's victory in one of the 125 qualifying races at Daytona International Speedway in Daytona Beach, Fla., in this February 1999 photo. Hutchens thinks about Dale Earnhardt all the time. "I don't think it will ever be the same," said Hutchens, director of competition for Richard Childress Racing. (AP Photo/Harold Hinson)

Already incredibly large in life, the persona of Dale Earnhardt became even larger after his sudden death.

Dale Earnhardt was 0 for his last 59 races everywhere—and, more importantly, 0 for his career at Daytona—when he finally won the 500 in 1998.

"Yessss! Yessss! Yessss!" Earnhardt exclaimed, pumping his left fist out of his car window as his black Chevrolet crossed the finish line. "We won! We won! We won!

"Twenty years . . ." Earnhardt added, the emotion of the moment evident in his voice.

After the 46-year-old Earnhardt finally crossed the finish line first in the 1998 Daytona 500, on his 20th try, pit crews from rival teams lined up along pit road to one by one slap The Intimidator's outstretched hand as he rolled triumphantly toward Victory Lane.

"I cried a little bit in the race car on the way to the checkered flag," Earnhardt admitted. "Well, maybe not cried, but my eyes watered up."

Appropriately, Earnhardt's long-awaited, long-overdue victory at Daytona came on the 50th anniversary of the first NASCAR race ever staged on the hard-packed sands of Daytona Beach.

After winning, Earnhardt drove into the grass in front of the main grandstand, spinning doughnuts, to the delight of the cheering crowd. When Earnhardt ascended to the press box for his postrace interview, his loyal fans gathered on the ground below, pulling up grass from where Dale had just spun and posing for pictures in their hero's tire tracks. Earnhardt waved down at them from the press box, and his followers joined hands to form a "3." Many dropped to their knees and began bowing toward their idol.

"The Daytona 500 tops 'em all," Earnhardt said, amusing the media by slamming down a little stuffed money that he had slyly concealed under his driving uniform. "I've got that damned monkey off my back!"

Dale Earnhardt's "Top 10 Reasons Why It Took Me 20 Years to Win the Daytona 500"—as enumerated on David Letterman's late-night show in 1998:

10. It took me 19 years to realize I had the emergency brake on.

9. Finally rotated and balanced my mustache.

8. Quit training with the Canadian snowboarding team.

7. Stopped letting my 300-pound cousin, Ricky, ride shotgun.

6. New strategy: Pretend I'm Dave driving home on the Merritt Parkway.

5. Who cares that it took me 20 years—at least my name isn't Dick Trickle.

4. Just figured out that if you mash the gas pedal all the way down, the car takes off like a son of a bitch.

3. My new pit crew: The Spice Girls.

2. This year, whenever I passed somebody, I gave 'em the finger.

1. My secret to success: One can of motor oil in the engine, one can of motor oil in my pants.

Winston Cup driver Dale Earnhardt, of Kannapolis, N.C., takes the checkered flag to win the Daytona 500 at the Daytona International Speedway on Sunday, Feb. 15, 1998, in Daytona Beach, Fla. It was his first-ever Daytona 500 win. (AP Photo/Phil Coale)

Cocky and daring, Dale Earnhardt burst onto the NASCAR scene as the circuit's top rookie in 1979. That year, team owner Ron Osterlund offered crewmen Jim Delaney and Lou LaRosa their choice of three drivers for the upcoming season: David Pearson, Cale Yarborough, or a relative unknown named Dale Earnhardt.

They both picked Earnhardt.

"Dale was cocky, he was a smartass, which is great," LaRosa recalled. "You've got to be aggressive. The cleaned-up image they have today for the drivers is bullshit. A race driver is like a boxer. How can you be a timid boxer? You have to be aggressive, determined and focused. You don't win races if you're not. [Earnhardt] didn't give a shit. He was going to the front."

Dale Earnhardt's late father, Ralph, had been a highly successful short-track racer in the Carolinas, where he struggled to make a living on the Sportsman circuit. But Dale, whose dad died when he was 22, arrived in NASCAR unheralded and virtually unknown.

In his first 125-mile qualifying heat at Daytona in 1979, the 27-year-old Earnhardt made a brazen, last-ditch run at established driving superstars Darrell Waltrip and A. J. Foyt before finally settling for fourth place. When Earnhardt climbed out of his unsponsored yellow and blue Buick, he looked at the reporters gathered near his garage and inquired, "How 'bout it, boys? Think I'm gonna make it?"

Leaving the track after the final race of the '79 season, Earnhardt passed a billboard that read: "Congratulations Richard Petty, Winston Cup Champion; Dale Earnhardt, Rookie of the Year."

"That ain't shit," Earnhardt sneered. "I want to be Winston Cup champion next year."

A year later, Earnhardt won his first of seven Winston Cup championships.

Dale Earnhardt drove briefly for Richard Childress late in the 1981 season. However, he wrecked so many cars that when Childress sat down to balance the books at the end of the year, he discovered Earnhardt's frequent crashes had left him $75,000 in the hole.

Reluctantly, Childress let Earnhardt go. Two years later, the two men hooked up again. Then fellow race car owner Bud Moore had just four words of caution for Childress. "Boy," Moore warned, "he'll break you."

The late Dale Earnhardt recalled the first time he laid eyes on Daytona International Speedway in 1976.

"I turned off I-95 and I could see the first turn behind the dog track," he recalled. "Then I could see the grandstand.

"I kept driving and driving and seeing more grandstands. It seemed like we drove forever and we couldn't get past the track. From the outside it was pretty intimidating."

Richard Petty won the Daytona 500 seven times. Dale Earnhardt won it only once. But The Intimidator "owned" Daytona. Over the years, he won 33 races other than the 500 at Daytona International Speedway. For 10 years in a row (1990-99), Earnhardt ruled Thursday's Twin 125 qualifying races. Andy Petree was Earnhardt's crew chief for three of those Twin 125 wins.

"Only thing we had to do was just buckle him in there," Petree recalled. "He was the man, I'm telling you."

"Ninety-nine percent of it was Dale Earnhardt," said Danny Lawrence, an engine man on Earnhardt's race team who was present for all 10 qualifying wins in The Intimidator's remarkable run. "He'd already won that race most of the time before he even went into it. He knew what he needed to do, knew where he needed to be. Where there was a will there was a way, and it was Dale Earnhardt who won all them races.

"Looking back at a lot of those years, we'd come to Daytona with new body styles, brand new cars, different engine rules, or different size restrictor plates. But no matter what they threw at him, he won that thing. It's amazing."

Even in defeat, Dale Earnhardt often overshadowed the Daytona race winner. That was never more true than in 2001, which shall forever be remembered as the year Dale Earnhardt died—not the year Michael Waltrip finally won his first race.

In 1990—the race he frequently referred to as "the Daytona 499"—Earnhardt, the prerace favorite, dominated until he blew a tire when he drove over a piece of metal bell housing off Rick Wilson's car one mile away from the checkered flag, opening the door for unlikely 32-year-old winner Derrike Cope.

Earnhardt lost the 1993 Daytona 500 when Dale Jarrett took advantage of a push from Geoff Bodine on the last lap.

"Big damn deal," growled The Intimidator, who had led for 107 laps. "We've lost this race about every way you can lose it. We've been out-gassed, out-tired, out-run, out-everything. We've not won it about every way you can't win it."

On the crucial closing laps in 1995, Earnhardt roared all the way from 18th place to 500 winner Sterling Marlin's rear bumper. But that was as close as he could get.

Earnhardt was running second with 11 laps to go in the 1997 Daytona 500 when his car got loose, brushed the wall, collided with Jarrett, and then flipped into the air. The feared black Chevrolet momentarily landed on its roof, then flipped again, back onto its wheels, before skidding to stop in the grass.

Earnhardt climbed out of his battered car and was about to enter the waiting ambulance for the ride to the infield medical center when he noticed that all four wheels on his Chevy were still intact. Earnhardt walked back to his car and asked the workman who was hurriedly hooking the No. 3 car up to the wrecker to "see if it will crank."

The car started and Earnhardt barked, "Get out of there. Give me my car back."

Earnhardt drove his crippled car back to the pits, where his crew taped things together enough to allow him to complete six more laps and finish in 31st place.

Almost every driver has favorite memories of Dale Earnhardt.

Rick Mast recalled the time he spun out and wrecked after colliding with Earnhardt. When Mast arrived at the track the following week for the next race, Mast was greeted by the strange sight of a man bent over from the waist, with his hands touching his toes—and his butt stuck up in the air.

"Go on and kick it," Earnhardt announced. "I know you wanted to."

On one of his first spring visits to Daytona for the annual 500, Dale Earnhardt was pulled over by the beach patrol for racing his four-wheel-drive truck on the sand.

"Where'd you learn to drive, boy?" the perturbed officer demanded to know.

"North C'lina, I guess," replied the grinning driver who sat slouched behind the steering wheel.

"The guy was just so comfortable in the race car," Jeff Gordon recalled. "When we were racing, any chance I got I'd look over to see what he was doing because he was always grinning or [giving a] thumbs-up.

"He was just a guy who loved what he did and he was so good at it he was able to enjoy it even at its most intense moments."

As a youngster, Kurt Busch was a huge Dale Earnhardt fan. A poster of The Intimidator hung on his boyhood bedroom wall. But as a rookie in 2000, Busch collided with Dale Earnhardt Jr. in a late-season race, and Kurt later heard rumors that Dale Sr. intended to settle the score on behalf of his son. As Busch waited to be introduced to the crowd prior to the 2001 Daytona 500, Earnhardt, accompanied by his wife Teresa and their daughter Taylor, walked by.

"Good luck, Mr. Earnhardt," Busch said.

Earnhardt ignored him.

Two-thirds of the way through the 2001 Daytona 500, Earnhardt let Busch know that he did, indeed, harbor a grudge. Coming out of the fourth turn, The Intimidator slid hard into the side of Busch's car. Then, just to make certain the kid got the message, Earnhardt raised his middle finger in salute.

Dale Earnhardt loved to play pranks on his fellow drivers. After Earnhardt put grease on the windshield wiper blades of Sterling Marlin's rental car, Sterling retaliated by attaching weights to the wheels of Dale's rental.

In a hurry to leave the track after a race in Sonoma, Calif., Earnhardt fumed as he was forced to drive 35 mph all the way to the airport.

Earnhardt insisted upon wearing an open-face helmet long after most drivers had switched to the full-face models that provide more protection. Over the years, other drivers, notably Rusty Wallace, had urged Earnhardt to make the switch to a safer helmet. When Earnhardt reluctantly agreed to try one in practice one day, he pulled back into the pits after one lap and disgustedly hurled the helmet out the window.

As Dale Earnhardt battled his way to 76 victories and more than $41.7 million in Winston Cup prize money, he emerged as both a hero and a villain in the eyes of NASCAR fans. Half of the people loved him. The other half feared Earnhardt's infamous black car and the supposedly sinister man inside.

In order to understand what drove Dale Earnhardt, it helps to know where he came from. Earnhardt dropped out of school in the ninth grade. "Failed a year, and quit," he would later explain.

Married at 17, Earnhardt soon fathered a son, Kerry. After his divorce, Earnhardt let his ex-wife's new husband adopt the boy. "I couldn't afford to make the alimony and child support payments," he admitted.

Earnhardt's second marriage resulted in a daughter, Kelly, and a son, Dale Jr. But Earnhardt's domestic situation didn't improve.

"I was borrowing five hundred dollars at a time on ninety-day notes from the bank just to race," he recalled later. "Maybe I should have gotten a regular job. Racing cost me my second marriage because of the things I took away from my family.

"For our family cars, we drove old junk Chevelles—whatever you could buy for two hundred dollars. We didn't have money to buy groceries. We probably should have been on welfare."

Earnhardt's second wife, Brenda, would cry as Dale drove off to race after race, towing his dirt car on a trailer.

"My wife wanted security," Earnhardt admitted. "We didn't have it. Everybody I knew was saying, 'Boy, you better git you a regular job.'"

In the sport's formative years, Dale's father, Ralph Earnhardt, was one of the best short-track racers in the South. He not only raced, he also built race cars for other people. There was precious little gold or glory in racing in those early years, especially in the mill town of Kannapolis, N.C., about an hour north of Charlotte.

As a youngster, Dale Earnhardt often rode alongside his dad in the family truck as Ralph towed his car to weekend races. Dale watched his dad work on his engines, hour after hour, week after week, year after year. As soon as he was old enough, Dale began sticking his own head under the hood, too.

Following in his father's footsteps—and ignoring Ralph's admonitions to stay in school—at age 18, Dale Earnhardt found himself a husband and a new father with no diploma, pumping gas and cleaning windshields for a living, with few real prospects for the future. What the young Earnhardt really wanted to do was race. Eventually Dale talked his way into a part-time ride. Ralph Earnhardt was his coach.

"He really didn't tell me how to drive or what to do," Earnhardt recalled years later. "But he showed me what happened when I did get in trouble. A guy wrecked me one night, and I remember Daddy saying, 'Well, you know, if you'd have just gone on and driven your race car—but you were checking up, trying to keep him from wrecking you. And you let him wreck you.'"

It was a lesson Earnhardt never forgot.

Long before he was old enough to trade paint on a race track, Dale Earnhardt honed his driving skills by racing slot cars. Young Earnhardt was a champion there, too. Years later, wealthy and successful beyond his wildest dreams, Earnhardt proudly produced the eight-inch plastic slot racing trophy that he had won as a teenager. Racing is racing.

Ralph Earnhardt preferred to pace himself until late in a race to protect his precious equipment. He liked to sneak up on opponents as they closed in on the checkered flag. The Intimidator was less calculating. His goal was to get to the front of the pack as quickly as possible—and then stay there.

He was arguably the best stock car driver since David Pearson—and certainly the most successful financially.

Sometimes smiling snidely, sometimes sneering, sometimes surly, Earnhardt knew only one way to race—"WFO," he called it.

That, for the uninitiated, stands for "Wide Fuckin' Open." When Dale Earnhardt first reached the big time, NASCAR's Winston Cup, he was broke. Worse, he owed $16,000 for tires and parts.

At the time of his death, Earnhardt's estimated gross annual income—from racing, merchandising, endorsements, sponsorships and appearance money—was approaching $100 million. Sources put his total worth at a half-billion dollars. Earnhardt had his own seat on the New York stock exchange as well as a 72-foot yacht, named *Sunday Money*, and a minor-league baseball team. He owned a Chevrolet dealership and 750 acres of farmland and real estate in North Carolina, where he kept registered black Angus cattle and quarter horses. He owned a Perdue farm with 32,000 chickens and had two full-time pilots on staff to fly his helicopter and two airplanes, a Lear jet and a King Air 200.

Not bad for a ninth-grade dropout.

The Crash

The sudden, tragic death of Dale Earnhardt made people who had never previously paid the slightest bit of attention to stock car racing sit up and take notice. His death captured the attention of this country in much the same way that the passing of Elvis Presley, Princess Diana and James Dean did. Suddenly, the hero of the recently provincial sport of stock car racing was on the same pedestal with entertainment heartthrobs and international royalty.

"The focus [Earnhardt's death] brought is totally unprecedented in the history of this sport," NASCAR vice president Jim Hunter declared. "We knew he was fairly famous. But we had no idea of the magnitude of his popularity and his reach. We discovered he was an icon."

Ironically, in the week leading up to the 2001 Daytona 500, Earnhardt had made light of the many injuries he had suffered while racing. Like many drivers, The Intimidator always felt indestructible.

A candle burns by a portrait of Dale Earnhardt outside Richard Childress Racing Enterprises Museum in Welcome, N.C., on Feb. 19, 2001. The NASCAR champion died from injuries suffered in a last lap crash during the 2001 Daytona 500. Richard Childress is the No. 3 car owner. (AP Photo/Gerry Broome)

"I drove with a broke leg, a broke collarbone, a broke sternum," Earnhardt said.

A year earlier Earnhardt had also complained about the lack of action and excitement at Daytona, suggesting that NASCAR founder Bill France Sr. would have been turning over in his grave from boredom.

Earnhardt disagreed with his fellow drivers who felt that the constantly tweaked Winston Cup cars were reaching speeds that were dangerously fast.

"If you're not a race car driver and not a racer, stay home," Earnhardt bristled. "Don't come here and grumble about going too fast. Get out of the race car if you've got feathers on your legs or butt. Put a kerosene-soaked rag around your ankles so the ants won't climb up there and eat your candy ass.

"How far can you go?" Dale Earnhardt asked rhetorically in the days leading up to the 2001 Daytona 500. "How far is safe? Should NASCAR have any guidelines on that?"

"I don't know," Earnhardt admitted, answering himself.

Days later, the world got an answer it didn't want to hear when Earnhardt, running in third place behind Michael Waltrip and his own son, Dale Jr., clipped Sterling Marlin, lost control of his car and hit the concrete wall head on.

"The only reason I won this race is Dale Earnhardt," admitted a subdued Waltrip, before he knew Earnhardt's accident had been fatal.

"I was so looking forward to doing well for him," said Waltrip, whose 0-for-462 career had been resuscitated during the off season when Earnhardt hired Michael to drive for Dale Earnhardt Inc.

"Then I got to Victory Lane and he wasn't there. He's not only my owner, he's my friend. It doesn't seem right."

Twenty-four hours before the 2001 Daytona 500, Dale Earnhardt and former Winston Cup champion Terry Labonte met in Dale's luxuriously outfitted million-dollar motor home, which was parked in the Daytona Motor Speedway infield, to plan an upcoming promotion for die-cast model cars. The advertising campaign was scheduled to commence in March. But when that date was mentioned, Earnhardt suddenly quipped, "That's if I make it that far."

As Labonte later recalled, everyone assembled for the meeting chuckled. Everyone except Dale Earnhardt.

Hours before the 2001 race, Jeff Burton, one of the more safety-minded drivers in Winston Cup, remarked, "I'm sure there will be a big wreck today. I just hope we're not in it."

A year later, Burton remembered Earnhardt, his departed friend and fellow driver.

"A person of that stature, you just don't think is going to be killed," Burton said. "It's a mental game that I think race car drivers play with themselves. When a young guy gets killed, it's 'Well, he wasn't strong,' or 'He didn't know enough about this,' or 'I wouldn't have done that.'

"When it happens to him, it's like 'Holy shit!' Now it hits home.

"My image is [Earnhardt] standing beside someone with his arm clenching their neck, because once he started to like you, that's what he'd do. He would walk up behind you and you would almost get knocked over by his arm, grabbing you and pushing you.

"He was the hard-headedest man in the world," added Burton. "But he was a neat guy."

On the fateful last lap, when Earnhardt tried to grab the inside groove, the rear of Dale's Chevy brushed the front of Marlin's Dodge. Earnhardt began swerving. As Dale struggled to regain control, he bumped Marlin again.

"I guess Dale thought he had us cleared," Marlin said later.

Out of control, Earnhardt's car slid up the track toward the outer wall, where Ken Schrader, who was riding the high groove, slammed hard into the passenger side of the famous black No. 3 Monte Carlo.

Earnhardt, with his seat belt improperly installed, without the protection of a head-and-neck restraint or a full-face helmet, struck the wall virtually head on at 160 mph.

"Everybody in racing died a little bit that day," Chip Ganassi, Sterling Marlin's car owner, said.

Many assumed Dale Earnhardt—who was battling Sterling Marlin and Ken Schrader for third place on the last lap of the 2001 Daytona 500—was trying to run interference for his son, Dale Jr., and eventual race winner Michael Waltrip, who drives for Dale Earnhardt Inc.

Not true, Schrader later insisted.

"Dale couldn't have cared less about protecting those guys," Schrader maintained. "He was worried about getting passed."

Indeed, on his car radio minutes before the start of the race, Earnhardt—who desperately wanted to win a record eighth Winston Cup championship—exhorted his pit crew: "Let's kick ass for this championship."

Watching the final moments of the race from the pits on that fateful Sunday, team owner Richard Childress didn't at first believe Earnhardt's crash had been that serious. He kept trying to contact Dale on his headset. But there was no answer.

"Dale would have raced the Daytona 500 if it paid two hot dogs and a Coke," Childress said later. "Dale wasn't racing for the money. He was racing because he loved to race. That's what he was doing on that [last] lap. He was racing."

Earnhardt's widow, Teresa, was prominent in Victory Lane when Dale finally won the 500 in 1998. And she was at Daytona in 2001 when Dale died.

Three hours later, she burst into tears at a nearby hospital when medical attendants sought to remove the wedding band from her deceased husband's finger. Attending physician Dr. James Bohannon convinced attendants to leave the ring on Earnhardt's hand.

Michigan State University biomechanical engineering professor Dr. Bob Hubbard was at Daytona International Speedway the week before the 2001 Daytona 500, urging drivers to wear his potentially life-saving Head and Neck Support system. As usual, the reception ranged from apathetic to skeptical.

Some of stock car racing's elite thought the device too confining or too uncomfortable. Others weren't sure that it would make that much of a difference in the event of a serious crash. Typically, most took a cavalier, macho attitude toward the recent rash of race track fatalities.

"You tend to get into this denial sort of thing," acknowledged Jeff Gordon. "We'd say, 'Oh, it won't happen to us.'"

Mark Martin looked at Dr. Hubbard's revolutionary U-shaped safety harness, turned his back, and walked away.

"I won't wear one of those devices for anything," the wiry Martin declared.

When the green flag waved at the start of the 2001 Daytona 500, only six drivers—out of the field 43—were wearing Dr. Hubbard's HANS harness, which he had developed in conjunction with his race car driver brother-in-law Jim

Race driver Jim Downing poses with a race helmet attached to a Hans Device Wednesday, Feb. 21, 2001 at Downing Atlanta in Chamblee, Ga. The device is designed to keep a driver's head from snapping forward in an accident. (AP Photo/John Bazemore)

Downing. Tragically, fan favorite Dale Earnhardt was not one of the six. Earnhardt had steadfastly refused to wear a head-and-neck restraint. He called the safety device "a damn noose."

When a speeding race car hits a concrete wall, the impact can exert more than 100 times the force of gravity. The seat and harness that were widely used in NASCAR were designed to hold the driver's body securely in place. But without a HANS or Hutchens device, the only things holding the driver's helmeted head in place were his neck muscles and his spinal column.

Dr. Robert Hubbard first began studying the mechanical properties of skull bone for his doctoral dissertation in college. He later helped develop crash-test dummy technology for General Motors in the mid-1970s. He also worked on his race car driver brother-in-law's pit crews.

"I've been interested in cars forever," Hubbard said. "I think I learned how to read by reading car magazines as a kid. I love cars."

Hubbard first began working on the concept of the HANS device in the early 1980s. He filed for his first patent on the restraint system in 1985.

"Jim [Downing] really was the guy who identified the basilar skull fracture as a problem for drivers," Hubbard explained. "Jim was the guy who identified the need for something that restrained the head during a crash.

"One of his friends had been killed in a crash in Ohio. The car went off the track on the backstretch and hit a dirt embankment. The car stopped, but the driver's head kept going. He suffered a skull fracture and he died.

"Jim was aware of other drivers who had probably died that way, but he didn't realize that was the most common way that drivers could go. And I happened to have a background in crash testing. Solving the problem became an avocation for me. Together, we set out to come up with a good way to reduce the risks."

In 1989, Hubbard and Downing conducted the first full-scale auto racing crash tests, complete with helmet and seat belts, that had ever been run in the U.S.

Using facilities at Wayne State University in Detroit, they strapped dummies, wearing the developing HANS device, onto sleds. "We're one of the pioneers," Hubbard said.

"There have always been a lot of people who recognized it as a good idea, something that would be useful," Hubbard said. "But people really didn't have good information to understand what their problem was.

"You've got to realize, the people who race—in fact, most people in general—don't have clue about what happens in a crash.

"It took time for us to develop credibility," Hubbard admitted. "We had several tests and various studies conducted by the different car companies, and they consistently said the HANS worked and was the right thing to do. But just because the experts said this was a great idea didn't mean it would work in the real world.

"It took a long time. There are a lot of decision makers in racing—the drivers, the teams, the sanctioning bodies, the sponsors and so on. We had to convince all of those guys that was the right thing to do. We had to develop a record of performance in the field."

Dale Earnhardt always wore Bill Simpson's safety equipment. The two men had met in 1978 and soon became friends. Before Simpson departed Daytona in February 2001 to watch the 500 at home in Indianapolis, he stopped by Earnhardt's motor home.

"Have a good race," Simpson said, shaking Earnhardt's hand. "I'll see ya."

Dr. Hubbard didn't bother to stick around Daytona for the 2001 race, either. Instead, he flew home to East Lansing, Mich., on Friday. Hubbard's work at Daytona was done.

"There was nothing more for me to do there," he recalled. "The guys don't want to talk to me about the HANS device once they put their game faces on."

Hubbard was cross-country skiing in northern Michigan on Sunday, Feb. 18, when Earnhardt—the indestructible Intimidator—lost control of his car on the last lap, within sight of the finish line, hit the concrete wall and lost his life.

Would Dale Earnhardt be alive today if he had heeded Dr. Hubbard's warning and worn the HANS device?

"Probably," Hubbard said somberly.

"There are lots of possible scenarios as to what happened to [Earnhardt] and his car. He had a lot of problems with that crash. The NASCAR report put their best guess out. With their best guess, or anybody else's best guess, if he had been wearing a HANS device, I'm pretty certain he would have survived."

A year later, in the accident-filled 2002 Daytona 500 won by Ward Burton, every driver wore either Dr. Robert Hubbard's HANS or the Hutchens device, designed by Richard Childress Racing Team engineer Bobby Hutchens. NASCAR, under fire in the wake of Earnhardt's tragic death, had made head-and-neck restraints mandatory.

Unfortunately, it took the deaths of Earnhardt, Adam Petty, Kenny Irwin, truck racer Tony Roper, and open-wheel drivers Greg Moore and Gonzalo Rodriguez—all within 17 months, and all, at least in part, from fractures at the base of their skulls—to convince the sport that something more than helmets and seat belts was necessary.

"It's frustrating to see a driver injured or killed when they didn't need to be," Hubbard said. "Gonzalo Rodriguez, Adam Petty, Dale Earnhardt . . . they didn't need to die.

"When NASCAR had the deaths of those younger drivers, and then Dale Earnhardt, that was a wake-up call for them."

"Because it was Dale," Jeff Gordon admitted, "it made all of us say, 'Wait a minute!' If it can happen to the best in our sport, it can happen to any of us."

Ask Richard Childress—who was a struggling race team owner trying to juggle his debts when Dale Earnhardt went to work for him in 1984—what kept him going after his star driver and good buddy was killed at Daytona, and he'll tell you about a hunting trip the two men took in the mountains of New Mexico. Childress fell off his horse and might have lost his life. Relaxing back at their cabin that evening and reliving the day's harrowing events, Childress told Earnhardt, "You know, if that had killed me up on that mountain today, you'd better went out and raced Phoenix [the following weekend]."

"Same deal here," Earnhardt replied. "You know, we've got to carry this thing on."

Childress recalled that conversation in February 2001, in the days after Earnhardt was killed.

"That Sunday night and Monday, all I wanted to do was think about getting away and quitting, getting totally out of the sport," Childress admitted.

"I laid awake both nights and thought about the things that Dale and I had talked about, and how we were going to go forward no matter what happened.

"If it was me, he was going to go forward, and if something happened to him, I was to go forward."

When Richard Childress decided, after a couple of soul-searching days, to keep on racing he immediately named Kevin

Harvick as his new driver. "There was no other name mentioned, no other name thought of," Childress said.

"If Kevin Harvick was going to be the future of Richard Childress Racing, then that's what we needed to do," crew chief Kevin Hamlin said.

Childress had hired Harvick to race his Busch series car in 2001. Earlier, there had been talk of Harvick possibly replacing Earnhardt someday, but neither Childress nor Earnhardt were certain that would be the right move. Their plan was to bring Harvick along slowly and see.

Suddenly, Harvick was called upon to compete on both the Winston Cup and Busch circuits full-time—and bear the tremendous burden of replacing the legendary Earnhardt as well. Out of respect for Earnhardt—and out of compassion for the inexperienced young Harvick—the No. 3 Chevy Monte Carlo was quickly repainted white and emblazoned with the number 29. But that did little to diminish the pressure Harvick felt.

Nevertheless, at Atlanta, in the third race of Harvick's stepped-up Winston Cup career—driving the same Monte Carlo that Earnhardt had piloted to victory in the same Cracker Barrel 500 a year earlier—Harvick out-dueled NASCAR superstar Jeff Gordon to claim the checkered flag.

As the two cars raced side by side toward the finish line, team owner Richard Childress—who had been one of Earnhardt's closest friends as well as his boss—looked toward the heavens.

"I looked up in the sky and said, 'We need your help, old buddy,'" Childress recalled.

"And he was there."

A nine-foot bronze sculpture of Dale Earnhardt, holding his 1998 trophy, his left fist raised high in the air in a victory salute, now stands outside Daytona International Speedway. Atop the wall behind the statue rest silicon replicas of Earnhardt's driving gloves and the lucky penny, given to him by a nine-year-old girl, that he mounted on the dash of his car for the 1998 race.

Hours before the start of the 2002 race, fans were lined up eight to 10 deep around the bronze statue of Earnhardt, quietly snapping pictures and whispering remembrances.

"Even though it is the year anniversary of his death," Bill Elliott noted, "Dale would have wanted us to go on."

A $4.2 million pedestrian overpass across International Speedway Blvd. now bears his name.

"I know we'll move on and the sport will continue to grow, but something will be missing," admitted Jeff Gordon, Earnhardt's archrival in Dale's later years. "It's definitely not the same, that's for sure."

Rusty Wallace, for one, doesn't think the tributes to Dale Earnhardt will subside any time soon.

"This is like Elvis," Wallace observed. "Here is it, 25 years later, and we're still commemorating Elvis Presley. I think Dale is gonna be no different. I don't think he's like a normal driver. I think he stands above and I think this is gonna go on and on. And there's nothing wrong with that."

The black skid marks that marred the concrete wall coming out of turn four at Daytona International Speedway at the conclusion of the 2001 Daytona 500—ominous reminders of the crash that had claimed the life of NASCAR icon Dale Earnhardt—were quickly covered with a heavy coat of white paint.

And in the wake of charges in some quarters that NASCAR was trying to whitewash and cover up the cause of Earnhardt's death, the sport underwent the most sweeping, safety-related changes in its 54-year history.

"NASCAR had to do something—and they did," noted Dale Earnhardt Jr., who remained a staunch NASCAR supporter throughout the controversy that swirled for months around his dad's death. Head-and-neck restraints, scorned for years by many NASCAR drivers, are now mandatory. "Black box" recorders, outlawed until 2002 because NASCAR feared crew chiefs might use the information garnered from the electronic gizmos to gain an advantage over competitors, are now mandatory in all cars.

NASCAR has approved new energy-absorbing, composite-fiber seats—much more rigid than earlier aluminum models, which could actually be bent with a person's bare hands. The harnesses that hold the drivers securely in their seats must now be installed according to the manufacturer's recommendations. The days of custom-fitted seat belts, such as the one Earnhardt was wearing when he died, are over.

NASCAR now requires all pit crew members to wear helmets and protective fire suits. In addition, NASCAR has opened two new high-tech research and development centers in an effort to develop safer cars.

"We've learned more in one year about safety, and acted upon it, than we had in the past 10 years," three-time Daytona 500 champ Dale Jarrett, an early advocate of increased safety measures, admitted in 2002. "We're much, much safer now than we were at Daytona a year ago."

I attended a media party at the Speedway three days before the 2001 Daytona 500. There another writer—a regular on the NASCAR circuit—pointed to the press credential hanging around my neck

"If he wins, that's going to worth a lot of money," my colleague noted.

"If who wins?" I asked, not having a clue as to what the guy was talking about.

The writer pointed again at my credential.

Only then did I realize that, out of the thousands of media credentials that were issued for the 2001 Daytona500, I had been assigned credential No. 0003.

Dale Jr.

He is the son of a legend, the grandson of a pioneer. He was bred to drive race cars; he was groomed to be great. He is backed by the big bucks of the biggest beer maker in this country. And he has the promotional clout and marketing might of NASCAR behind him. Is it any wonder Dale Earnhardt Jr. has been an instant success?

"I feel almost like I'm cheating a little bit—getting in here while the getting is good," Dale Jr. admitted.

Growing up in his famous father's shadow, young Dale Jr. never understood why his dad was gone so much.

"I was always saying, 'Where are you going? Why do you have to go? Don't go. Stay home.' I never thought about it happening to me. I probably should have."

Although Dale Earnhardt and Dale Jr.'s mother, Brenda Jackson, divorced when the youngster was two, you couldn't miss the pride in The Intimidator's eyes whenever he looked at his son. When Dale Jr. was six years old, he left his divorced

Dale Earnhardt Jr. celebrates in Victory Lane after winning the NASCAR Pepsi 400 Saturday, July 7, 2001, at Daytona International Speedway in Daytona Beach, Fla. (AP Photo/ Peter Cosgrove)

mother's side to move in with his dad. The elder Earnhardt immediately stuck his son in a go-kart.

"Right off, I hit a telephone pole," Dale Jr. recalled. "My dad just laughed."

One day, Earnhardt put his son in a race car and told him to drive.

"He didn't tell me anything else," Dale Jr. remembered. "I even had to learn how to put it in gear by myself."

Later, Earnhardt would wrap his arm around Dale Jr.'s neck and make typical fatherly admonitions about sleeping too late or listening to the wrong kind of music. Dale Jr. knew it annoyed his dad when he stayed out half the night and then slept late the next morning. So, like all kids, that was exactly what he did. He knew that next to racing, his dad loved hunting and fishing. So Dale Jr. made it a point to tell a reporter in an interview how much he hated to hunt and fish.

"I had this little bit of brat in me somewhere," the young Earnhardt admitted after the tragic crash. "That's all gone now."

Dale Earnhardt Jr. was streaking across the finish line at Daytona in his bright red Chevrolet in 2001 even as his famous dad was dying on the race track, half a mile behind him. He was the sentimental favorite to win the Daytona 500 in 2002. People expected Junior to carry on The Intimidator's tradition of seven championships and 76 wins. But it took the legendary elder Earnhardt 20 years to win the Daytona 500. It was unreasonable to expect Dale Jr. to do it in three.

Nevertheless, when Junior appeared at a bookstore across the street from Daytona International Speedway, people began lining up at 4 a.m.—a full 14 hours before Earnhardt was scheduled to appear.

"He may have 'Junior' behind his name, but he's got just as much skill and talent as his father had," rival Tony Stewart declared. "He drives like Dale Earnhardt Sr. He's got all the talent in the world."

Meanwhile, Dale Earnhardt Jr. continued to insist the 2002 Daytona 500 was just another big stock car race.

"Nobody really seems to get it," he maintained. "I like being here. This track will always have a special place in my heart. This was where my father died."

Junior may have made his peace with Daytona International Speedway, but the famed asphalt oval certainly didn't show any compassion for Junior in the 2002 Daytona 500. In a series of unfortunate incidents, Earnhardt blew his right front tire, blew his right rear tire, lost his brakes, went speeding through the frontstretch grass, and got caught up in a fiery 18-car crash.

"It got real dirty, that was the only bad thing," said Earnhardt, who was forced to settle for 29th place, 29 laps behind the winner, Ward Burton. "But overcoming the flat tires and being competitive, that was cool. And sliding through the infield at 160 miles an hour with no brakes and no rear tire, that was cool. A lot of neat things happened this weekend."

Junior still wears his baseball caps backwards and cherishes his collection of CDs. But part of the playful little boy in Dale Jr. died Feb. 18, 2001 at Daytona, along with his dad. Since then, he has had to grow up in a hurry—at 180 miles per hour.

"Some of the aspects of racing that were huge to me a year ago, don't really matter anymore," Earnhardt admitted later that summer.

"He's a special kid," said rival driver Kenny Schrader.

More than anything, Dale Jr. craved his famous father's approval. He raced, he later admitted, to make his dad proud. Suddenly that element was lost.

"When I was 10 or 15 years old, I would sit there and watch Dad race and think, 'Man, he gets to do that for a living and gets paid for doing it,'" Earnhardt recalled. "I guess I'm doing it now like everyone else is. Just out here to make a living."

There are no more father-son chats before each race. But Dale Earnhardt Jr. knows many of his father's fans have transferred their allegiance to him.

"It just seems like yesterday he and I were fishing on Lake Norman," the elder Earnhardt once said of Dale Jr. "He was a kid and had a big Irish setter named Rocket. And we were just having fun. It seemed like, boom, he's messing with race cars. Boom, he's driving 'em. And lo and behold, he started winning races. It seemed like it happened overnight."

And then, without warning, Dale Sr. was gone.

Wonder Boy

Dale Earnhardt looked like a stock car driver. Jeff Gordon doesn't. Sterling Marlin sounds like a stock car driver. Jeff Gordon doesn't. Gordon looks and sounds like he belongs in a church choir.

Only on a racetrack, with four wheels under him and the gas pedal pushed hard to the floor, does the real Jeff Gordon emerge: fearless, hard-charging, and extremely talented.

The then twenty-five-year-old Jeff Gordon showed the world what kind of driver he was going to be when he raced below the yellow blend line at the end of pit road to pass Bill Elliott and grab the lead with six laps to go in the 1997 Daytona 500.

"I would have gone down there to the people cooking out in the infield if that was what it took to get by Elliott," Gordon admitted later. "That was my last chance. That was the chance to win the Daytona 500 right there. And it paid off."

Jeff Gordon signs autographs for fans.(AP Photo)

The move made Gordon the youngest winner in Daytona 500 history and gave Hendrick Motorsports a one-two-three sweep with Gordon teammates Terry Labonte and Ricky Craven, who had both shot past Elliott on the outside to finish right behind Jeff.

"I was dead meat and I knew it," Elliott admitted. "With three Hendrick cars behind you, you ain't got a chance."

Two years later, Gordon employed a similar daring pass to slip by Rusty Wallace and set up a 10-lap showdown with Dale Earnhardt that resulted in Jeff's second Daytona 500 victory. Gordon's duel with Earnhardt on the final 10 frantic laps of the 1999 Daytona 500 will long be remembered as one of racing's great battles.

"That was the longest 10 laps I've ever run around Daytona," Gordon acknowledged afterwards.

Earnhardt tried to pass Gordon on the inside. Thwarted there, he tried the outside. Then he tried the inside again.

"I just couldn't get there," Earnhardt admitted with a mixture of admiration and disgust.

"I had a mirror full of black," Gordon said. "And that black car is not what you want to see on this race track. Keeping that car behind me was one of the toughest things I've ever had to do. He kept trying to get me. And I thought for sure he was going to. He came at me, big-time.

"I've got to thank Dale Earnhardt for making it what a great race it was. To race Dale Earnhardt down to the finish line for the Daytona 500 was a dream come true. To beat a guy I learned so much from, a guy I looked up to, a guy who has been as good as he has been at this race track, makes winning Daytona even sweeter.

"When I first came to Winston Cup in 1993, Dale was 'The Man.' And he still is, as far as Daytona is concerned."

On the cool-down lap, after the two cars had sped across the finish line with Jeff Gordon in front and Dale Earnhardt barely one-tenth of a second behind, the No. 3 car caught up with the No. 24 entering the first turn. There The Intimidator pulled alongside the rainbow-colored Chevrolet and gently banged the side of Gordon's Monte Carlo.

"He gave me a little 'doughnut,' and then he waved," Gordon said, grinning. "He wanted to put his mark on my car before it goes on display at Daytona USA. I think it was his way of congratulating me. Beating Earnhardt like that in the Daytona 500 is probably the biggest single thrill I've had."

"Give Gordon credit. He beat me," Earnhardt said.

Jeff Gordon, of Pittsboro, Ind. (24) beats Dale Earnhardt, of Kannapolis, N.C.(3), to the checkered flag to win the Daytona 500 Sunday afternoon, Feb. 14, 1999 at the Daytona International Speedway in Daytona Beach, Fla. (AP Photo/Glenn Smith)

Although the two men were often depicted as exact opposites and fierce rivals on the race track—it was Dale Earnhardt who hung the somewhat contemptuous tag "Wonder Boy" on Jeff Gordon—the bond between the two drivers actually ran much deeper than most people ever imagined.

"I like hunting and fishing—he likes those video toys," Earnhardt once growled. However, unbeknownst to the fans in the grandstands, the rough and gruff Earnhardt was actually the mild-mannered Gordon's unlikely mentor.

"No one will ever know how much time he spent with me during my first two seasons," Gordon admitted at Daytona as he prepared for the 2002 race. "He started out to be a guy I learned from, and he turned into the guy I knew was going to be my toughest competitor, especially at Daytona. He was so awesome here. He was always the guy to beat. If you beat him, you knew you accomplished something far greater than you could ever imagine. And if you got beat by him, you knew you got beat by the best.

"I remember running second behind Dale [Earnhardt] late in the race in my first Daytona 500 [1993]," Gordon said. "I didn't have a clue as to what I was doing—or what I was going to do. That was why I finished fifth."

When NASCAR legend Dale Earnhardt's life was suddenly snuffed out at Daytona in 2001, Jeff Gordon—so different from craggy-faced Earnhardt in so many ways, and yet so much like him in so many others—inherited the mantle of stock car racing's leading ambassador. It is not a role Gordon would have coveted—especially not earlier in his career. In fact, Gordon never wanted to be a stock car racer, period.

"I never thought I would win one Winston Cup race," Gordon admitted.

When Jeff was growing up, open-wheel racing appeared his likely career path. As Gordon graduated from quarter-midgets to go-karts to midgets to sprint cars, all anyone wanted to talk about was the annual Indy 500.

"Everybody I was racing would say, 'Indy 500, Indy 500,' and it got embedded in my head: 'Indy 500,'" Gordon recalled. "They have film of me doing an interview when I was eight years old, saying I wanted to win the Indy 500 someday."

Growing up in Southern California, Jeff had never even heard of the Daytona 500 or NASCAR. However, after his

Daytona 500 Champion Jeff Gordon, from Pittsboro, Ind., holds up a sign in Victory Lane, Feb. 16, 1997, at the Daytona International Speedway in Daytona Beach, Fla. The three Hendrick-owned cars finished 1-2-3. (AP Photo/Chris O'Meara)

first day of driving stocks cars at the Buck Baker Racing School in North Carolina, Gordon phoned his stepfather, John Bickford.

"This is what I'm going to do for the rest of my life," Jeff declared. "This is it!"

Jeff Gordon didn't become a champion race car driver overnight. He became one over many nights. He started racing competitively when he was five years old and spent many nights curled up in the back seat of his stepfather's car, returning home from another race in another town. At Bickford's urging, young Gordon competed in as many as 150 races a year. Gordon had eight or nine cars at his disposal and regularly raced quarter-midgets fifty-two weekends a year, winning every title and trophy he could find. By the time he was nine he was regularly whipping kids twice his tender age.

"We actually had some people in Phoenix who thought I should be prosecuted for child abuse. I took Jeff's whole childhood away from him," Bickford later confessed. "I had to fire him a couple of times to bring him around."

Gordon won the national quarter-midget championship in 1979 when he was eight years old. He won the title again when he was ten. By the time Gordon was thirteen he was racing sprint cars against grown men.

"I know I wouldn't be where I am without all those races I was in when I was younger," Gordon said. "If you're really dedicated and really focused and you want to get to the highest level, you have to start young and you have to work hard."

When Gordon was fifteen, the family moved from California to the Indianapolis area where there were no age restrictions to hold the talented youngster back. On the Midwest dirt tracks, Gordon quickly learned how to interpret the feel of his tires, and how to keep his car under control when those tires lost their grip.

"When I was young and racing the sprint cars, which are light race cars with high horsepower, I learned where the edge is and how to take the car to that extreme edge and not go over it," Gordon explained. "The sign of a good race car driver is being aggressive enough, but feeling where that edge is."

When Gordon was twenty-one, NASCAR team owner Rick Hendrick gave him a job. Most drivers on the circuit wait five years or longer before they are invited to drive for such a big-time owner with top-notch equipment and crew. Twenty-one-year-old rookie Jeff Gordon rewarded Hendrick's faith in him by winning one of the Twin 125s at Daytona in 1993.

"Oh my God! I can't believe it! Yesssss!" Gordon shouted as he crossed the finish line.

Then Gordon had to ask directions on how to get to Victory Lane.

There in Victory Lane, the mustachioed young Gordon met a twenty-three-year-old model named Brooke Sealey, a Miss Winston, who a year later would become his wife. NASCAR drivers and Miss Winston models are not supposed to mingle, so Gordon and Brooke had to date on the sly.

In the garage area, rivals—unaware of Gordon's clandestine relationship with Miss Sealey—thought it strange that the good-looking, up-and-coming young driving star never seemed to have a date.

At one point, Earnhardt bluntly asked Gordon if he was gay.

Many hard-core NASCAR aficionados resented Jeff Gordon, especially during his early years on the Winston Cup circuit. He was booed and hung in effigy, primarily because he was too good, too soon. He was seen as a pampered prima donna, a pretty boy who had his success handed to him on a silver platter.

But although he is usually depicted as clean-cut and almost cherubic, Gordon can put on a black hat once in a while, too. After the often reckless Robby Gordon (no relation) nudged Gordon's car out of the way in a race at New Hampshire, Jeff made a run at Robby during an ensuing yellow caution period and clobbered his car from behind. Publicly outraged—but probably secretly pleased at Gordon's unexpected show of anger—NASCAR officials sent Jeff to the rear of the pack for "rough driving."

"I gained more fans from what I did at New Hampshire than I did for winning the championship," Gordon admitted. "Hey, I got mad, there's no doubt about that. But I had people tell me, 'That was just great!' I thought it was awful. I lost control. But people said, 'It's okay to lose control once in a while. It shows you're human.' I had people who didn't pull for me say, 'Hey, man, I liked that. I'd like to see more of that.' And I said, 'If somebody rubs me the wrong way, you're going to see more of it.'

"We need a guy in black," Gordon continued. "But you can't make yourself that type of image. It has to be in you. Dale [Earnhardt] didn't just wake up one day and say, 'I'm going to be The Intimidator.' That was just the way he drove the car. In my mind, I'm a different kind of person. But I see this sport in some ways getting more physical. As it gets more competitive, it pushes us to be more physical with one another on the race track. However a guy races me, that's how I race him back. Most guys race me pretty clean because they know I race them clean. But if a guy bangs on me, he's gonna get it back.

"My first approach is to do it the right way," Gordon explained. "My second approach is do whatever it takes."

How much do you pay for car insurance? Jeff Gordon pays more than $100,000 a year.

"The cost is astronomical, but you have to have it," said Gordon, who declined to reveal how much his policy is worth.

"Insurance is something a driver cannot do without," agreed Geoffrey Bodine, who was nearly killed in a crash in the annual truck race at Daytona in 2000. "We all think we are invincible, but we are not."

In 1993, Jeff Gordon's rookie year, team owner Rick Hendrick phoned Darrell Waltrip, who had successfully bridged the gap between Richard Petty's reign and the emergence of Dale Earnhardt, to seek his opinion of Gordon.

"What do you think of the kid?" Hendrick inquired.

"He ain't gonna make it," predicted Waltrip, never at a loss for words. "He wrecks too much."

All In the Family

The history of stock car racing is filled with famous families, from the Flocks and the Allisons to the Pettys and the Waltrips, from the Bodines, Burtons, and Jarretts to the Labontes, Wallaces, and Earnhardts.

Obviously, stock car racing gets into the blood and into the genes.

Ralph Earnhardt—Dale's daddy, Dale Jr.'s granddaddy, and an outstanding racer in his own right—initially financed his budding racing career by building and fine-tuning motors for North Carolina auto shop owner Berl Eddleman, who supplied the horsepower for some of that area's most elusive moonshine runners in the 1940s.

All agree that the elder Earnhardt, who won more than 500 races of one sort of another in his lifetime, was as good a mechanic as he was a race car driver. As a rule, however,

Eddleman's mechanics, including Earnhardt, refused to work on police cars. A man has to stand by his principles, after all.

Tweaking the hot rods of others only served to fuel Ralph Earnhardt's own racing dreams. At every opportunity, he volunteered to test the fine-tuned Fords that he had been working on over the one-mile course that had been measured off on the country highway not far from the repair shop. Flying down the road at 120 mph made all the hours Earnhardt had spent bent over under those hoods seem worthwhile.

Ralph Earnhardt soon became a regular on the North Carolina short track circuit. One of his principal rivals was Robert Yates, current owner of NASCAR's No. 88 and No. 28 cars. Yates owned the only race car in the area that had a spoiler on the rear deck lid. And race after race, Earnhardt would go out of his way to ram the rear end of Yates's car in an effort to damage that spoiler. In addition, Earnhardt frequently accused Yates of cheating. In those days, it cost $100 to protest the results of a race. Whenever Yates won, Earnhardt would convince 13 or 14 of his similarly suspicious friends to ante up $10 apiece. Earnhardt would then post the $100 in protest money—and put the balance in his pocket.

There have been Pettys in NASCAR for as long as NASCAR has been in existence, and they have been big names in Daytona since before the Speedway opened. Lee Petty raced on the beach before winning the inaugural Daytona 500 in 1959, and son Richard, The King, picked up right where Lee left off, winning the 500 a record seven times.

"I've been coming here too long to have a memory. I've been coming down here [to Daytona] with my father since I was born. Kids remember things like Disney because they go there twice in their life. I've been coming here twice a year for the last 41 years," explained Kyle Petty, son of Richard and grandson of Lee, about his family's connection to Daytona.

Eleven-year-old Richard Petty was in the audience on June 19, 1949 for the inaugural race in NASCAR's new "Strictly Stock" division, which would later become Winston Cup. Lee Petty borrowed a friend's prized '48 Buick Roadmaster, and with wife Elizabeth and sons Richard and Maurice following behind in the family car, drove to Charlotte, N.C., for the race. Once there, the elder Petty proceeded to roll the borrowed car over four times in the race, seriously damaging the hood, roof and fenders. While Lee made arrangements to have the wrecked Buick towed back to Level Cross, N.C., Elizabeth and Maurice drove home in the family car. Young Richard, who had remained behind to console his dad, had to hitchhike home alone because there was no room for him to ride in the wrecker.

Lee Petty won a 1954 beach race in Daytona after Tim Flock, who featured one of NASCAR's first two-way radios in his car, was disqualified for using an illegal carburetor. Petty had driven to Daytona in a 1953 Dodge that he intended to enter in the race. But when he got to Daytona, Petty purchased a new 1954 Chrysler New Yorker. He removed all the racing paraphernalia from the Dodge and installed it on his new Chrysler. When the race was over and Petty had been declared the winner, he told his young son, Richard, to drive the Chrysler home to North Carolina. Flock was so angry at the disqualification that he didn't race again the rest of that year.

Lee Petty regularly made a habit of protesting the results of races that he didn't win. At Atlanta in 1959, after he had

Kyle Petty, center, holds the trophy with help from his grandfather Lee Petty, left, and father, Richard, second from right, as the Petty family celebrates in Victory Lane in Daytona, Fla., after Kyle's first racing win in this 1979 photo provided by the Richard Petty Museum. (AP Photo/HO, Petty Enterprises)

been upstaged in a race by a grinning young kid, Petty protested that he, not the youngster, had actually finished first and that, in the heat of the action, the other driver had mistakenly been credited with one extra lap.

A quick check of the scoring sheets proved Lee Petty correct. The victory was immediately taken away from the stunned kid—whose name happened to be Richard Petty.

"I didn't really question it since it was family," recalled Richard, years after he had been "robbed" of what would have been his first victory. "I guess I'd still be there arguing about it if it was someone else."

As famous as the Pettys became, there was no doubt that their family roots were buried in the soil that sprouted NASCAR itself—the soil of the country South.

"The Pettys lived out in the country," early NASCAR competitor Ralph Moody once noted. "They grew up that way. They only talked to people they knew. If they didn't know them, they shut their mouth. They didn't talk about people, didn't say anything, good or bad or anything else. It was nobody's business."

In 2001, in a race that was forever marred by the tragic last-lap death of Dale Earnhardt, Darrell Waltrip's younger brother Michael won the Daytona 500, snapping a personal 16-year, 462-race losing streak. Prior to his victory at Daytona, Michael Waltrip had only finished as high as second once in his career. Ironically, Michael's victory came on the same day that his talkative brother Darrell made his debut as a Fox TV commentator.

As a teenager, Geoff Bodine, a moody hotshot driver from upstate New York—hardly traditional NASCAR territory—had taken home movies of the Daytona 500 from the back end of the family station wagon parked in the infield. By 1986 Bodine was another of Winston Cup's up-and-coming young stars.

Bodine won the Daytona 500 that year when Dale Earnhardt, who was waiting to make a last-lap, last-ditch run at Geoff, ran out of gas. Bodine's mother and father, Carol

Geoff Bodine, from Chemung, N.Y., gives a victory signal on Friday, February 13, 1987, in Victory Lane after winning the International Race of Champions at Daytona Speedway. (AP Photo/Kathy Willens)

June and Eli, had spent the day selling their son's souvenirs out of trailer parked across the street from the race track. After Geoff celebrated in Victory Lane and was debriefed by the press, he went over to the family trailer to sign autographs and help peddle his own souvenirs.

When Geoff Bodine spun but failed to hit anything during the 1986 Busch Clash prior to the Daytona 500, NASCAR president Bill France Jr. called him "Mr. Lucky." Little did anyone realize how prophetic those words would prove to be. In 2000, Bodine was nearly killed at Daytona in a spectacular, fiery truck race crash.

Bodine later claimed that he had come so close to death in the moments immediately after the accident that he actually spoke to his deceased dad.

"I told him I was coming to see him," Bodine said. "And he said, 'No, it's not time yet. There's more to do.'

"Looking at the remains of my truck and the video, I'm totally convinced that's what God did," Bodine continued. "He sent my father down here to save me from that wreck as a guardian angel."

Two days later, Bodine tried to watch the Daytona 500 on TV from his hospital bed, just down the street from the Speedway.

It wasn't easy. "I had a lot of morphine in me," Bodine said.

In 2001, Geoff Bodine traveled to Daytona in February strictly to offer advice and encouragement to his brothers, Brett and Todd. But he refused to go to the track to watch the big race.

"I couldn't bring myself to come to the race track on Sunday morning," Bodine admitted. "It wasn't because of the traffic jams, either. It's very hard to be there and not be in the Daytona 500."

In 2002, Geoff returned to Daytona International Speedway and not only raced in the 500 but finished a surprising third behind Ward Burton and Elliott Sadler.

"I'm not over the hill yet," said the 52-year-old Bodine, "I still have my nerve. I didn't have anything to prove. But, hopefully, this proves that I am back. Professionally, [the 2000 truck crash] changed my career. It was a struggle there for a while. It puts a lot of things in perspective, a perspective of good and bad, and what's important and what's not so important.

"I had a near-death experience. There's a closeness, the way I feel, a closeness to God. I wouldn't change that. I'd do it over again if I knew that was going to happen."

When Brett Bodine finished 22nd in the first of two 125-mile qualifying heats in 2001, he assumed he had missed making the Daytona 500 field for the second year in a row. Only the top 14 finishers in each qualifying race are guaranteed spots in the main event. And after his 35th-place finish in the points standings the previous season, Bodine knew he didn't have much of a chance at getting one of the seven provisional starting spots in the 500. Brett was so distraught he jumped into his personal car and headed south on Interstate 95 as fast as he could go.

"I just knew we missed it and I didn't want to be around anybody," Bodine explained. "I wanted to handle it myself."

Bodine, who was listening to the second 125-mile qualifier on his car radio, had reached Cocoa Beach, about an hour away, when the second heat ended. He pulled into a convenience store, bought a soda and a bag of potato chips and began sorting through his slim chances of sneaking into the 500 via a provisional. Minutes later, his wife Diane, who was back at the track, called on Bodine's cell phone to say Winston Cup officials had just announced that he had indeed been awarded the 43rd and final spot in the fabled race.

"This is my whole life," admitted Bodine, who took advantage of the opportunity and finished 15th in the 2001 Daytona 500. "This is my family's whole life. People have no idea what this life is like. People have no idea the emotional roller coaster. How much my family pours their hearts and souls into this.

"I mean, this means $100,000, just to make the race. To lose $100,000 in income to us is huge, just huge. Thank the Lord we're not in that tailspin right now. The plane has leveled off before we hit the ground."

Bodine collected $133,509 for his 15th-place finish in the 2001 500.

The presence of the three Wallace brothers—Rusty, Kenny and Mike—in the 2002 Daytona 500 marked the third time the trio had made the race, breaking the old record of two previously shared by the Wallaces and the Bodine brothers—Geoff, Brett and Todd.

"In this business, you learn that blood is thicker than water," Mike Wallace observed. "My mom was walking up to people saying, 'You know how many boys I got in the Daytona 500? Three of 'em. All of 'em.'"

The Jarretts

Dale Jarrett shot past Johnny Benson on a restart with four laps to go, then held off Jeff Burton, Bill Elliott, and Rusty Wallace with the help of another yellow flag two laps later to win his third Daytona 500 in 2000, in a decidedly dull race.

But four hours earlier, Jarrett wasn't even certain he would be participating in the big race at all. The lights in Jarrett's garage had burned until 10 p.m. on Saturday night—long after the other drivers and crews had returned to their motor coaches and motel rooms. While the other 42 race teams rested and plotted strategy, Jarrett's crew worked frantically to put Dale's No. 88 Ford Taurus back together again. If NASCAR officials had let them, they would have worked all night. The next morning, race day, they were back at it at 4:45 a.m., while the competition was still fast asleep, dreaming of checkered flags.

All week during practice, Jarrett had avoided the large packs of cars that drafted with one another on the track. He

Dale Jarrett, center, poses with his family after winning the NASCAR Winston Cup Series championship Sunday, Nov. 14, 1999, at the Homestead-Miami Speedway in Homestead, Fla. Jarrett finished fifth in the Pennzoil 400 race to clinch the championship. From left, his father, two-time Winston Cup champion Ned, Jarrett's daughter Karsyn, 9, Jarrett's mother Martha, Jarrett, Jarrett's daughter Natalee, 11, Jarrett's son Zachary, 5, Jarrett's wife Kelley and Jarrett's brother Glenn. (AP Photo/Alan Diaz)

knew he had a strong car and didn't want to risk damaging it. Finally, after one last adjustment on Saturday afternoon, Jarrett had gone out on the track to see how his car would react in traffic. Then a senseless fender bender involving Jarrett, Jeff Gordon and Bill Elliott in the waning moments of Saturday's "Happy Hour" practice session had left the blue body of Jarrett's

Taurus looking more like a vehicle on the lot at Rent-A-Wreck than the car to beat in the Daytona 500.

"The front end was wobbling all over the place, pretty much every corner of the car was damaged," admitted Jarrett's crew chief, Todd Parrott. "The car took a pretty hard lick. [The collision] bent all the rocker panels and the back bumper. The nose was pushed up about a half-inch. All the exhaust pipes, both sides, and half the rear bumper was flattened."

"Knowing the time and effort it takes to make one of those cars go fast, I felt we had pretty much taken the race out of our hands," Jarrett conceded.

Three body repair specialists from Jarrett's race shop in Charlotte, N.C., rushed by jet to Daytona overnight. Fully 40 percent of the body had to be replaced—and the crew had less than seven hours in which to do it.

The 42 other cars in the race had already been lined up along pit road for more than an hour when Jarrett's weary workmen finally pushed his Ford out of the garage and into the pole position—a scant 30 minutes before the green flag. The paint was still wet on the two new front fenders. Parrott, who had gotten less than four hours' sleep, fretted that the freshly applied sponsors' stickers, so vital to a team's continued financial success, might blow off in the breeze. Jarrett himself worried that his rebuilt car wouldn't navigate the Speedway's four corners.

"I didn't know what to expect," Jarrett admitted. "Did we get the front end back together right? Was it going to stick to the track? I wanted to make sure the car was going to turn."

Hours later, as Jarrett rolled down pit road following his traditional victory lap—only the fourth driver to win as many as three Daytona 500s—Richard Petty, another of that fabled four, trotted over to Dale's car with his right hand extended.

"That sent chills up my spine," Jarrett admitted. "To think that The King would come out to congratulate me."

Ned Jarrett, former driver and TV commentator and father of Dale, began racing in the early 1950s under the assumed name of "John Lentz" because his own dad frowned on auto racing. Known as "Gentleman Ned" in a fledgling sport that in its early, formative years was filled with scoundrels, Jarrett won the Winston Cup championship in 1961 and 1965—a feat duplicated by his son, Dale, in 1999.

Unlike his son, Ned Jarrett competed in seven Daytona 500s without ever winning. Ned missed his best chance in 1963 when he ran out of gas and finished third behind Tiny Lund.

Ned Jarrett's NASCAR career earnings totaled $289,146. Dale collected four times that amount on one afternoon when he won the 2000 Daytona 500.

"I felt stock car racing had a tremendous amount of potential, but nothing like we've seen it come to now," the elder Jarrett admitted. "I could never imagine my son or anybody else winning a couple of million dollars for winning a race."

Ned Jarrett once won a race car in a poker game. Today it costs more than $100,000 to build a decent race car and millions more to keep it running all year.

"In 1957, I agreed to buy a '57 Ford for $1,800," the elder Jarrett recalled. "But I had no money. So I waited until the banks closed on Friday and I wrote a check, knowing there were two races coming up that weekend that paid $950 each to the winner. If I won them both, I could cover that check Monday morning."

Although one race was in Myrtle Beach, S.C., and the other was in Charlotte, N.C.—and drivers didn't jet around in private planes in those days—Jarrett somehow won both events.

Dale Jarrett took advantage of a "push" from Geoff Bodine on the last lap to slip past Dale Earnhardt and win the 1993 Daytona 500.

Upstairs in the broadcast booth, Jarrett's dad urged his son on.

"C'mon, Dale," Ned Jarrett exhorted over the air. "Go, baby, go!"

The victory—NASCAR's biggest—was new team owner Joe Gibbs's first as a stock car owner.

In 1996, Dale Jarrett again beat Dale Earnhardt at Daytona, powering his way to victory when Earnhardt couldn't find anyone to draft with him. On this day, Jarrett simply had the stronger car.

"The Fords were too strong, man," grumbled The Intimidator, who had lost the stock car sport's biggest race in three of the previous four years—to Jarrett twice and Sterling Marlin—by a combined margin of .89 seconds.

"What [Earnhardt] didn't have," Jarrett bluntly noted, "was a Robert Yates engine."

Bobby Allison
and Sons

Three-time Daytona 500 winner Bobby Allison bought his first race car at a junkyard for $600. He went on to win 84 Winston Cup races. Only Richard Petty (200) and David Pearson (105) ever won more. Bobby was first driver to earn more than $100,000 in a Winston Cup race and was voted NASCAR's most popular driver six times. He passed his name and his racing legacy on to his two sons, Clifford and Davey, but sadly, that name is now associated with a frightening amount of tragedy, the most ever to be visited on any one prominent racing family. Before the traumatic deaths of Clifford and Davey, however, racing was definitely all in the family, and at Daytona, the Allisons knew how to make their name shine.

"I grew up with the Allisons," said Robert Yates, who was Bobby's engine builder at DiGard Racing and later owned Davey's No. 28 Ford. "A driver's confidence rubs off on the crew and how you work with the crew. When we went to

Davey Allison, left, of Hueytown, Al. talks with his father Bobby Allison after a practice round June 18, 1988 at the Miller High Life 500 NASCAR race at Pocono International Raceway in Long Pond, Pa. (AP Photo/Russ Hamilton)

Daytona with an Allison, we knew we had the driver department covered. They understood the draft. They loved it. They knew this was our big event. They ate it up."

In addition to the banner events, Bobby Allison also loved to race on the many minor-league short tracks around the country. During the middle of the week, between NASCAR races, he would pilot his own airplane and participate in as many races as he could.

"It is," he explained, "my golf game."

Bobby Allison knew mostly frustration in his first 14 Daytona 500s. Although he finished second in 1975, he was a full lap behind winner Benny Parsons. Finally in 1978 the breaks went 40-year-old Bobby's way, and Allison—zero for his last 67 NASCAR races and zero for 14 at Daytona—won his first 500.

"We had our share of luck to get here today," Allison admitted.

Many agreed that it was about time.

In 1981, unhappy with the way his Oldsmobile was handling during testing after NASCAR had downsized its cars in response to the country's energy crisis, Bobby Allison secretly switched to a Pontiac LeMans prior to the Daytona 500. Allison's crew chief, Waddell Wilson, aware that the LeMans was on NASCAR's list of approved vehicles, noticed that the rear roof on the LeMans was not as steeply sloped as the Olds and thought that might make a difference.

The Ranier Racing team worked feverishly to get the new car ready for Daytona. When Allison won the pole, reaching a speed of 194.624 mph, rival teams cried foul. But NASCAR ruled that Allison had done nothing wrong. He would have won the 500 that year if he had not run out of gas on the 174th lap and been forced to coast nearly half a lap into the pits. Even so, Allison fought back into contention and finished second, 3.5 seconds behind Richard Petty. A month after the 1981 Daytona 500, NASCAR revamped the spoiler on Allison's Pontiac, negating the advantage he had enjoyed.

Bobby was driving a Buick the following February. But even in victory in 1982, Allison was engulfed in controversy.

His rear bumper fell off his car, apparently as a result of a light tap from Cale Yarborough on the fourth lap, causing a five-car pile-up. Yarborough's crew chief Tim Brewer immediately claimed that the bumper had fallen off by design. Other observers agreed that the two cars had not appeared to actually touch at all.

After Dale Earnhardt's engine blew a head gasket, Allison—running without a rear bumper—battled Darrell Waltrip and Joe Ruttman. When Waltrip, who held the lead, blew an engine, Allison charged out in front. He ran out of gas just as he streaked across the finish line, more than 22 seconds ahead of Cale Yarborough. Bobby had to get another splash of gas just to get his triumphant car into Victory Lane. But though the checkered flag ended the race, it did not bring a halt to the raging "rear bumper controversy."

The day before the race, NASCAR director Joe Gazaway had ordered Bobby Allison's crew chief Gary Nelson—who is now the managing director of racing competition at NASCAR—to lower the rear bumper on Allison's car by one-quarter of an inch.

"Gazaway always had some sort of problem with me," Allison recalled. "He walked up to us and said, 'I want that back bumper moved. You guys are cheating. That bumper ain't where it's supposed to be. You move it right now or you don't go on the track for Happy Hour.'"

When Allison and Cale Yarborough collided early in the race, Yarborough's front bumper supposedly hooked Allison's recently reattached rear bumper and tore it loose. The bumper fell off, several other speeding cars struck it or swerved to miss it, and Joe Millikan hit the wall.

Immediately rumors spread that Nelson had rigged the bumper—which in those days was a 25-pound piece of metal—

to fall off during the race. It is a story that Nelson adamantly denies to this day.

"I knew right from the start I had the strongest car," Allison insisted. "I knew, if nothing happened, the race was ours."

The last of Alabama hotshot Bobby Allison's 84 Winston Cup victories—and one of his most dramatic—came in the 1988 Daytona 500 when Bobby's son Davey, a chip off the ol' block, finished right behind him in second place. Though it was the first one-two father-son finish in Daytona history, it was not the first such finish in NASCAR history. In 1959, Richard Petty and his father Lee finished one-two in Atlanta. But Lee protested, and the results were reversed. The following year they did it again, this time with Lee actually leading Richard across the finish line.

As usual, Bobby Allison didn't cut his son any slack as they raced toward the checkered flag. Nevertheless, an emotional Davey later called it the most memorable moment of his career.

"This," Davey declared, "is the happiest day of my life. It's better than if I had won myself. He's always been my hero."

"What a thrill, seeing Davey in my mirror and knowing we were going to sweep it," Bobby remarked moments after the race ended. "I'm proud to say that Davey is mine."

Unfortunately, Bobby Allison now has no memory of that magical moment. One of the accidents that took so much from the Allison family also robbed Bobby of his memory.

In June of 1988, the elder Allison crashed after blowing a tire on the first lap in a race at Pocono. He was broadsided by Jocko Maggiacomo and driven into the wall. As the race continued under caution, Davey Allison drove lap after lap past the sickening wreck for 20 minutes while his dad lay unconscious in his crashed car, near death with massive head injuries and a shattered left leg. Davey kept racing and finished fifth.

At the hospital that evening, a doctor pulled Davey Allison aside and warned, "If your daddy lives through the night, he'll probably never be able to do anything again."

Bobby Allison did recover—but his life was never quite the same.

"I was going along, doing really, really great—and then I woke up in a hospital bed," Allison recalled. "I didn't know what year it was and I didn't know what state I was in.

"I went through such a long period where I hurt so bad and things didn't make sense to me," Allison continued. "I had an awful lot of pain that just wouldn't seem to go away. Then there was the confusion and all. I've gone through years of rehab that includes an incredible amount of memory loss. To this day, I still have some horrible memory loss."

While Bobby Allison struggled to regain his health, he immersed himself in the racing career of his youngest son, Clifford. "Then," Bobby recalled, "we had the tragedy with Clifford."

Clifford Allison was killed in a wreck at Michigan International Speedway in 1992 when he struck the wall while practicing for a Busch race. Bobby was there. He walked up to Clifford's car on the track, where his son lay inside, dead.

"When I walked up to that car and saw that boy was dead—knew that boy was dead—there began a pain I never had known before," the elder Allison said. "And it kept hurting."

In the wake of that tragedy, Bobby Allison turned his attention to his other son, Davey, already a highly successful Winston Cup driver.

"Davey said, 'Come on, Dad, come with me,'" Bobby recalled. "I knew Davey enjoyed having me around and we enjoyed doing this together. And then we lost Davey."

Davey Allison was killed in July 1993 when the helicopter he had purchased a month earlier and was still learning how to fly crashed in the infield at Talladega. Allison was trying to land in a parking lot near the garage area when he clipped a nearby 12-foot-high chain-link fence, ripping the tail section off the helicopter. He died in the hospital the next morning, 11 months to the day after his brother Clifford was killed.

"Let me tell you the real irony of life," Bobby Allison would say years later. "Davey worked, worked, worked all his life, from the time he was a little bitty guy. He was so focused on what he wanted to do and what he wanted for a career.

"Clifford played, played, played. You could not get him to be serious. He was a good young boy and talented at mechanical things, but he would not devote himself to anything.

"Clifford played, played, played—and got killed working.

"Davey worked, worked, worked—and got killed playing.

"I don't think life has to be fair," Allison continued. "And I don't think life is fair to a lot of people. I've had lots of good times. I've had some bad times, too. But at least I had the opportunity to have those good times."

Bobby Allison, rival driver Darrell Waltrip once noted, "is the only man in racing I can walk up to and just start crying."

Davey Allison, who in 1987 became the first rookie ever to start the Daytona 500 on the front row, won 19 Winston Cup races in his tragically abbreviated eight-year career, including the 1992 Daytona 500. That victory occurred after Sterling Marlin and Bill Elliott, who were both driving for Junior Johnson at the time, crashed midway through the race while battling for the lead. Reportedly, Junior was so angry over the accident that he refused to speak to Marlin for the rest of the year.

That wreck, involving nine of the 16 cars on the lead lap, opened the door for Allison, who was not seriously threatened for the rest of the afternoon. And Allison did it in his backup car, after crashing his primary Ford in practice earlier in the week.

"We didn't dream of winning the race," admitted Allison's team owner Robert Yates. "But after Junior's cars wrecked each other and another good car, Michael Waltrip I think, ran out of gas, we said, 'Here we go.'"

Thus, Bobby and Davey Allison joined Lee and Richard Petty as the only father-son combinations ever to win the 500. However, that 1992 Daytona 500 victory still ranked as only the second biggest day of Davey Allison's career.

Victory, he always insisted, "was not as special as finishing second to my dad."

The Brawl

Young Dale Earnhardt made his Daytona 500 debut in 1979. But he had already caught the eye of many race fans with his impressive seventh-place finish in the Firecracker 400 at Daytona the previous summer. Lap after lap, Earnhardt raced around the track on Donnie Allison's rear bumper until finally he had to pit for fuel, leaving Cale Yarborough to fight it out—quite literally—with Allison and his brother Bobby. Yarborough and Donnie Allison bumped several times while battling for the lead on the backstretch of the final lap, ultimately knocking one another out of the race.

That's when things really got exciting.

As the race continued to its conclusion, the two drivers climbed out of their Oldsmobiles to continue the personal confrontation. They were exchanging insults when Allison's older brother Bobby, still seething over an earlier encounter with Yarborough, pulled up alongside the wrecked cars and inter-

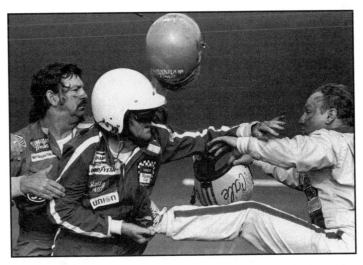

Bobby Allison holds race driver Cale Yarborough's foot after Yarborough kicked him following an argument February 18, 1979 when Yarborough stopped his car during the final lap of the Daytona 500. Allison's brother Donnie was involved in a wreck with Yarborough on the final lap, which made brother Bobby stop. (AP Photo/Ric Feld)

jected himself into the discussion. When Yarborough slapped at Bobby Allison with his helmet, bloodying his face, Bobby climbed out of his car.

"How Bobby got out of that car that fast, I'll never know," Donnie said later. "But I knew what was going to happen. I'd seen that look on Bobby's face before. I kept yelling at them, 'We're on national television!'"

Helmet in hand, Donnie Allison, who was normally more easy-going than Bobby, came to his brother's defense—but not before Bobby had punched Cale in the face two or three times.

"All of a sudden," Bobby Allison explained later, "Cale's nose was pounding on my fist."

Yarborough took a poke at Donnie and tried to kick Bobby, who in turn lunged at Yarborough's leg and hoisted it into the air.

Meanwhile, Richard Petty took advantage of NASCAR's rule that allows drivers to continue to race for position until the start/finish line under a yellow caution to grab the checkered flag for his sixth win at Daytona.

"As I came around after the race ended, it looked like Saturday night at a quarter-mile track in the old days," Petty snickered.

That was first Daytona 500 ever carried live from start to finish on national TV. And the impact on NASCAR, from mainstream American viewers, was similar to that which pro football experienced as a result of the sudden-death championship game between the Baltimore Colts and New York Giants in 1958. It was a pivotal moment, both for the sport and for the Daytona 500.

Until then, stock car races, including the annual Daytona 500, had usually been edited to condense the action, and carried days later, often on ABC's *Wide World of Sports,* along with ski jumping, checkers, and curling. But the 1979 nationwide TV audience, enlarged by snowstorms that gripped much of the country that weekend, certainly got its money's worth.

The three drivers were fined $6,000 apiece. But the widespread press coverage, which showed Donnie Allison standing behind Bobby, waving his helmet in the air, led to death threats against Donnie—even though he was the only member of the trio who didn't throw a punch in the melee. Donnie Allison, who never won the Daytona 500, never won another race.

Cale Yarborough

Crew chief Waddell Wilson was understandably proud of his record of four consecutive Daytona poles with Buddy Baker (1979, 1980), Bobby Allison (1981), and Benny Parsons (1982). So he couldn't understand why his new driver, Cale Yarborough, couldn't seem to get his car up to speed during practice for the 1983 Daytona 500.

"I had worked and worked and worked, but I couldn't get it to go any faster," Wilson later admitted. "I couldn't sleep."

What Wilson didn't know was that Yarborough was sandbagging, setting up the unsuspecting competition for Sunday. Cale eventually turned in a 200.503 mph qualifying lap at Daytona in 1983 but hit the wall and flipped his Chevy Monte Carlo upside down on his second lap, forcing him to surrender the pole to Ricky Rudd and climb into his year-old backup Pontiac Grand Prix for the race.

During the race, while chatting with CBS television announcer Ken Squires via an audio connection in his car,

Cale Yarborough (AP Photo)

Yarborough patiently bided his time until the last lap, when he passed both Buddy Baker and Joe Ruttman for the win.

"It's like a checkers game," Yarborough told Squires. "You put yourself in the right spot and you can win the game."

Yarborough was once again the fastest qualifier in 1984—and this time it counted, as Cale was clocked at a record 201.848 mph. From there he went on to become the first driver since Fireball Roberts in 1962 to win the pole, his qualifying race and the Daytona 500—all in the same year. Again Yarborough waited until the last lap to make his move, shooting past Darrell Waltrip on the backstretch.

"I didn't see a car out there all day that I couldn't pass when I wanted to," Yarborough boasted after chalking up his fourth victory in the fabled 500.

In his first Daytona 500, in 1962, Cale Yarborough finished dead last behind Fireball Roberts. On his way home, Yarborough had to borrow 35 cents to get across a toll bridge.

Unprecedented speeds in excess of 185 mph suddenly became commonplace during practice for the 500 in 1968, with David Pearson leading the way at 190.746 mph.

"I can feel the G forces stretching the skin of my face," admitted race winner Cale Yarborough when asked how it felt to go 185 mph. "It seems like my arms weighed about 100 pounds apiece and my head about 200 pounds."

Cale Yarborough was a staunch supporter of Jimmy Carter when Carter campaigned for the presidency in 1976. So outspoken was Cale, in fact, that NBC's new hit comedy show, *Saturday Night Live*, mentioned the two men together in a skit.

Cale Yarborough, from Timmonsville, S.C., sets off a Victory Lane shower with a bottle of champagne after winning the Daytona 500 auto race February 19, 1984. (AP Photo/Chuck Luzier)

In 1977, Cale Yarborough became just the second driver to win the Daytona 500 twice. Unusually high winds whipped up sandwich wrappers and other pieces of paper, blowing the debris onto the race car grilles of several top contenders, which in turn caused them to overheat.

"A win makes up for a lot of losses," Yarborough declared in Victory Lane.

As a youngster growing up in rural South Carolina, William Caleb Yarborough was bitten by a rattlesnake. Several days later, young Cale found a dead snake under a bush.

"I reckon after that snake bit me, he just crawled off and died," Cale observed.

"Cale was one of the toughest characters I've ever seen," said fellow driver Paul "Little Bud" Moore. "I don't think he had the God-given talent of a Bobby Isaac. But the only thing Isaac and myself could do was drive a race car. Cale could do anything. He could wrassle, play football, play softball. He excelled at all of them.

"Cale could endure anything, racing with broken steering, or kicking the flames under his feet. I've seen his face blistered, his feet blistered. They just don't come any tougher than that. Cale was as tough as Dale Earnhardt, and that's saying something."

Awesome Bill From Dawsonville

Bill Elliott, the Huck Finn lookalike with the head of bushy red hair and the thick Georgia accent, won the pole for the Daytona 500 in 1985, breaking Cale Yarborough's year-old speed record with a mark of 205.114 mph.

"I guess I was pretty close to what they call 'the ragged edge,'" Elliott admitted after his record run. "At times it [his Ford] felt out of aerodynamic control. At that point, I was just riding it. I wasn't driving it."

Elliott was equally dominating in his 125-mile qualifying heat, winning and leading 48 of the 50 laps. After that, Darrell Waltrip was heard to declare, "Boys, the handwriting is on the wall."

"It's sure a long way from when we came here in 1977, ran 170 mph, and didn't make the field," Elliott admitted.

But Elliott's qualifying run was only the beginning. Driving a red Ford Thunderbird that was clearly the fastest car in the field, Elliott won the 1985 Daytona 500 with ease as de-

Bill Elliott (AP Photo)

Bill Elliott, from Dawsonville, Ga., gets a victor's reward in Victory Lane February 15, 1987 after winning the Daytona 500 auto race (AP Photo/Walt Chernokal)

fending champion Cale Yarborough and key rivals Neil Bonnett, Bobby Allison, Dale Earnhardt, A. J. Foyt, David Pearson, Benny Parsons, Terry Labonte and Harry Gant all blew their engines trying to catch him and NASCAR's king, Richard Petty, lost his clutch.

"Ten years ago, when I started racing, if they had told me I'd win this race and this much money [$185,500], why, I would have told them that they were nuthin' but a big ol' liar," a beaming Elliott proclaimed.

But Bill Elliott's sudden success and popularity came with a stiff price for someone who had grown up far from the limelight. He was constantly hounded by the media, sponsors and new-found fans. Police officers had to be posted in his garage to keep the prying press and pestering public away.

"All I ever wanted to do was race," Elliott said sadly. "I never knew it would be like this."

Bill Elliott's victory in 1985 signaled a changing of the guard in NASCAR and at Daytona. The era of Richard Petty, David Pearson, Cale Yarborough and A. J. Foyt was over. The age of Elliott, Dale Earnhardt, Rusty Wallace, Mark Martin and Geoff Bodine had arrived.

When Geoff Bodine ran out of gas with three laps to go in the 1987 race, Bill Elliott won his second Daytona 500.

"We couldn't outrun Elliott, so we had to try to outlast him," explained Bodine, who eventually ended up in 14th place.

In 1987, NASCAR instituted a new rule, limiting pole qualifying attempts to one lap. And Bill Elliott was immediately clocked at 210.364 mph—a Daytona speed record that still stands.

"One lap at that pace around here is all a man can stand," Elliott said.

Jaws

Millions of stock car fans who today enjoy Darrell Waltrip's clever quips and comments on TV may not appreciate the fact that he once was the boldest, winningest, most reckless driver in NASCAR. Everywhere except in the Daytona 500.

Unlike Buddy Baker, who kept coming close in the 500 but seemed jinxed for so long, Waltrip couldn't seem to do anything right at Daytona. Although Darrell finished a surprising 12th in his 1973 Daytona debut, more often than not Waltrip struggled in NASCAR's No. 1 race. When Richard Petty crossed the finish line first in 1979, he could see Waltrip in his rear view mirror, waving his arms with joy—because he had finally finished second.

By 1989, Darrell Waltrip had accomplished just about everything in NASCAR that a man possibly could. In 17 years, he had won 73 races and three Winston championships. His quick tongue and his aggressive driving style had combined to

Darrell Waltrip (AP Photo)

make him stock car racing's biggest star. But still Daytona's checkered flag eluded him.

Finally, in 1989, Lady Luck smiled on Darrell Waltrip at Daytona. Convinced he couldn't outrun teammate Ken Schrader, Waltrip gambled and stayed out on the track when the other leading contenders pulled into the pits one last time for gas during the closing laps. With three laps to go, Waltrip grabbed the lead. But his fuel pressure light was blinking. Waltrip was certain he was running out of gas.

"It's out! It's out!" he screamed to his crew chief, Jeff Hammond, over his car's radio. "The fuel pressure is zero!"

"Shake it, baby, shake it," Hammond shouted back, exhorting his driver to swerve his car back and forth to splash the remaining ounces of fuel out of the tank.

It worked. "It's okay now," Waltrip announced. "The fuel pressure has picked up. It's going again. I can make it."

As his car cross the finish line, more than eight seconds ahead of Schrader, Waltrip got on his radio again.

"I won the Daytona 500! I won the Daytona 500!" he screamed. "This is the Daytona 500, isn't it? Don't lie to me! I'm not dreaming, am I?"

Rival drivers were understandably suspicious. After all, Waltrip had raced the final 53 laps—132.5 miles—on one tank of gas.

"I'd sure like to see that gas tank," third-place finisher Dale Earnhardt growled.

NASCAR agreed and took a look at Waltrip's tank, but discovered nothing illegal.

They also found virtually no fuel.

"For $5," one observer remarked wryly, "I'd drink what was left."

Darrell Waltrip celebrates in Victory Lane after winning the Daytona 500 in this Feb. 19, 1989 photo in Daytona Beach, Fla. (AP Photo/Doug Jennings)

At the time of his victory in '89, Darrell Waltrip was driving the No. 17 car and making his 17th start in the Daytona 500. His daughter, Jessica, was 17 months old. And eight and nine, of course, add up to 17.

In the second 125-mile qualifying race in 1981, Darrell Waltrip pushed past Benny Parsons coming off turn four by driving down to the apron of the track. An angry Parsons later charged Waltrip "was going to crash 12 cars" if Benny hadn't lifted off the throttle.

Several other drivers, most notably Richard Petty, agreed. "Darrell done one of the stupidest things today I've ever seen anybody do in almost a quarter-century of racing," Petty declared.

Several times, Waltrip's car was knocked out by blown engines at Daytona. In 1983, he was simply knocked out himself, suffering a severe concussion in one of the most serious crashes of his brilliant career. That wreck altered Waltrip's outlook on racing. He realized it sometimes might be smarter to play it safe than to later be sorry. To this day, Waltrip does not even remember the race he ran at Richmond the week after his 1983 wreck.

Darrell Waltrip was leading the 1984 Daytona 500 on the final lap when Cale Yarborough shot past him.

"I knew what was going to happen," Waltrip admitted later. "I didn't see no need of getting worried about it. On the last lap, I was thinking second."

Then Dale Earnhardt caught Waltrip just before the finish line, relegating him further back to third place. But Darrell was not about to complain.

"They had to carry me out of here on a stretcher last year," he said. "So I'm happy."

Darrell Waltrip frequently referred to himself as "D.W." Soon, others did too. Cale Yarborough, however, called him "Jaws," because Waltrip's mouth often ran as fast as his cars did. In his younger years, when NASCAR still felt the need to hustle customers, Waltrip would stand in the open doorway of his motel room at night and trade quips with people passing by.

"Are you with the show?" the curious would sometimes ask.

"I am the show," Waltrip would reply.

Jocko Flocko

One of the early heroes in the NASCAR beach races was Tim Flock, a renowned showman who sometimes raced with a live monkey, "Jocko Flocko," sitting on his shoulder.

Tim Flock was the star of the family, but his brothers, Fonty and Bob, and his sister Ethel also raced in NASCAR. All four Flocks competed in a Winston Cup race in the 1950s, and Ethel finished ahead of her three brothers. The Flocks inherited their nerve from their father, Carl, who was a circus tightrope walker.

Tim Flock was comfortably leading late in a NASCAR race on Daytona Beach in 1951 when he suddenly realized he was running out of gas. There were no radios in the cars in those early days, so Flock had no way of letting his pit crew know what he needed. So he drove unannounced back to his pit.

"The pit crew was drinking. I mean they were all drinking, celebrating our victory," Flock recalled. "When I pulled in, they didn't know what the hell was happening."

Stock car racer Fonty Flock straps on his helmet as he poses on the beach-road course at Daytona Beach, Fla., Feb. 26, 1956. (AP Photo)

Tim Flock won the 1954 beach race in Daytona, but Bill France disqualified him for using an illegal carburetor. Flock was so enraged that he refused to race again for the rest of that year.

He returned to Daytona the following February, strictly to watch the race and drink beer with his buddies. But Carl

Kiekhaefer, owner of a new white Chrysler 300, offered him a ride. Flock resisted at first because the car had an automatic transmission. "No car in the history of NASCAR has ever won at Daytona with an automatic transmission," Flock protested. "Don't worry about it," Kiekhaefer said.

Flock finished second behind Daytona hometown hero Fireball Roberts. But again Bill France disqualified the winner. This time Tim Flock was the beneficiary.

Carl Kiekhaefer was a major force in NASCAR in those early years. In addition to Tim Flock, Kiekhaefer tried to hire as many other top drivers and mechanics as he could. In Daytona, Kiekhaefer rented an entire motel and quartered his drivers and crew members at one end of the building, and their wives and girlfriends at the opposite end. No sex the night before the big race, Kiekhaefer ordered. "That was his rule," Flock recalled. "We were like boxers. And he would watch all night long. If you didn't play by his rules, you were fired the next morning."

Each day, at 6 a.m., Kiekhaefer would blow a whistle— the signal for his drivers and crew members to meet him out front of the motel. It was time to go to work.

Bill France Sr. personally banned Tim Flock for life in 1961 after Flock refused to renounce his support for a proposed drivers' union that would have been part of the Teamsters.

"No known Teamster can compete in a NASCAR race, and I'll enforce that with a pistol," Big Bill declared.

The union, which would have provided pensions, health and life insurance, and improved safety conditions for the drivers, was busted when prominent drivers Fireball Roberts and Ned Jarrett, among others, withdrew their support. Then, as now, stock car drivers were considered independent contractors, not employees of NASCAR or of the various race tracks.

Ironically, when Flock died of cancer in 1998 without medical insurance or money, Darrell Waltrip took up a collection among Winston Cup drivers so that Flock's widow wouldn't lose the family home.

The ill-fated union was partially the work of Curtis Turner, another free-spirited former driver and struggling race track owner. Reportedly, under the terms of a secret deal with union leader Jimmy Hoffa, Turner was to receive a much-needed $800,000 loan from the Teamsters. In addition, Turner was also supposed to convince NASCAR to allow pari-mutuel betting on its races. Along with Flock, the flamboyant Turner— who finished 13th and 7th in the first two Daytona 500s— was banned for life by Bill France.

Earlier, during secret negotiations, Curtis Turner invited NASCAR pioneers Fireball Roberts, Buck Baker and Tim Flock to fly with him in his private plane to Detroit to meet with Jimmy Hoffa and discuss the proposed union. When the quartet encountered bad weather en route, Baker began to get nervous.

"Hand me that fifth [of whiskey] I put in the plane before we left," Baker requested.

"What fifth?" Roberts replied.

Fireball and Flock had already consumed the entire bottle of booze themselves.

The Silver Fox

Despite David Pearson's successes on other superspeedways, the Daytona 500 had long been his Achilles Heel. Although Pearson won driver's championships in 1966, '68 and '69, he had been upstaged, especially in the Daytona 500, by Richard Petty. In 16 trips to Daytona during the month of February, Pearson had one second-place finish, a third, two fourths, a fifth and two sixths to show for his efforts.

In 1976, in one of the most famous Daytona 500s ever, the two rivals were racing for the checkered flag entering the homestretch on the final lap when Petty's Dodge drifted up the track and clipped Pearson's Mercury.

"The bitch hit me!" Pearson shrieked over his two-way car radio.

"He hit my left front fender with his right rear, and when he did, it just spun him right around and me too," Pearson later explained.

Pearson veered to the right, into the wall, while Petty fishtailed for a moment and then also struck the outside barrier. Both cars ended up in the grass.

After winning the first 125-mile qualifying race at the Daytona International Speedway, February 20, 1969, David Pearson is kissed from both sides in Victory Lane. (AP Photo)

"We tangled up and wrecked, but I managed to mash the clutch in and keep the engine running, which he didn't," Pearson said.

As Petty's out-of-control car spun toward the finish line, Richard found himself thinking, "I'm going to be the first to win the Daytona 500 backwards." Then Petty slid to a stop in the grass, 30 yards short of the checkered flag. Meanwhile, Pearson, with his engine still running, was on his radio again, screaming, "Where's Richard? Where's Richard?" In all of the smoke and confusion, Pearson couldn't see Petty's car. Pearson quickly got his own vehicle turned around and pointed in the direction of the checkered flag. At barely 30 miles an hour, Pearson's wrecked car limped across the finish line. As he passed Petty's vehicle, which was stalled in the grass, Pearson looked over and smiled. It was the 89th victory of Pearson's distinguished career—and probably the most precious of them all.

When angry members of Petty's pit crew reached his disabled car, Richard told them, "If you're going to blame somebody, blame me. There wasn't enough room for the move I made." As Pearson made his way to Victory Lane, Petty, who was walking back to the garage, shouted an apology to David for colliding with him.

"I've been waitin' a long time for this one," Pearson said. "He had me beat until we wrecked. I knew the only way I could pass him was to draft by him. I didn't know if I had enough power to do that."

"I had one ulcer before the race," quipped Petty, whose pit crew manually gave his car a push to try to get it started again. "Now I've got two."

David Pearson participated in his first Daytona 500 in 1960.

"It was a lot different from running a quarter-miler on dirt," he recalled. "I was used to throwing my arm out the window and waving to the guys behind me when there was a wreck. There was a wreck in the 500 and I did that, and the wind blowed my arm back against the quarter panel. I felt like I broke my arm. That was the first and last time I ever did that."

Pearson and Richard Petty were archrivals. From 1973 to 1977, the legendary pair finished one-two 63 times—with

Pearson winning 33 of those duels. In all, Pearson won 105 times. Only The King ever won more.

Although Pearson, a 10th-grade dropout, could be witty and outgoing when surrounded by friends, he lacked Petty's knack for dealing with the public and the press. As a result, "The Silver Fox"—as the cool and calculating, prematurely gray Pearson was known—never received all of the credit that he rightfully deserved.

"I was bashful," he admitted. "I would hide from the media, and Richard would talk to them. It hurt me in the long run. Richard did it the right way."

Pearson's penchant for privacy was legendary. He once owned a huge peach orchard in his native South Carolina. But when Pearson saw dozens of migrant workers, who had been hired to harvest his peaches, walking around on his property, he dismissed the strangers and cut down all of his peach trees. When Richard Petty retired in 1992 he was given a rousing send-off. But when Pearson departed in 1986, few uttered a word. One who did was Petty himself.

"Pearson could beat you on a short track," The King observed. "He could beat you on a superspeedway. He could beat you on a road course. He could beat you on a dirt track. It didn't hurt so bad to lose to Pearson because I knew how good he was."

People said Pearson was superstitious. David always denied that. Returning home in the evening, if Pearson saw his neighbor's black cat crossing the street in front of him, he would stop his car, back up, and drive around the block in order to approach his house from the opposite direction.

"I'm not superstitious," he insisted. "I just don't want to take no chances."

Junior Johnson

Junior Johnson, a hard-charging North Carolina moon-shiner who had spent 11 months in a federal penitentiary in Ohio, arrived in Daytona in February of 1960 with a race car that had been hastily assembled just seven days earlier. The Chevrolet was owned by John Masoni, who also owned the dog track that still operates, overshadowed by today's massive grandstands, outside the first turn at Daytona International Speedway. Masoni had paid noted auto mechanic Ray Fox twice his normal fee to put together a race car at the last minute for the 1960 Daytona 500.

Johnson, who preferred Pontiacs, was ready to turn around and go home—"I about decided that I was wastin' my time," Junior later admitted—when he discovered the secret to drafting at Daytona. That was precisely what Johnson was doing when either a gust of wind or the suction created by Johnson's Chevy inexplicably blew the rear window out of Bobby Johns's Pontiac with nine laps to go.

Junior Johnson peers from his car after winning the pole position for the Dixie 400 stock car race at the Atlanta International Raceway, June 3, 1964. Johnson qualified for the $56,000 race with a four-lap speed of 145.906 miles per hour. (AP photo/str/xn)

"It was one of the damnedest things I ever saw on a race track," Johnson admitted.

Johnson blew by Johns and finished 23 seconds in front for the biggest win of his colorful career.

Junior Johnson was one of the most notorious of NASCAR's early moonshining drivers. As a youngster, Johnson had to climb over cases of illegal whiskey at night just to get into bed.

"I never drove at Daytona as fast as I'd driven on Highway 421, comin' out of Wilkesboro," Johnson once confessed.

Federal revenue agents first raided the still of his father, Robert Glenn Johnson Sr., in 1935, when Junior was four years old. On one such raid, agents destroyed more than 7,000 cases of booze.

When Johnson was 14—not yet old enough to legally drive to church—Junior was hauling his daddy's illegal hooch to market in a 1940 Ford.

"Growing up hauling moonshine, about all the roads was dirt," Johnson recalled. "You didn't have no paved roads out in the country. So I learned to drive dirt very, very good because that's where I'd go when I wanted to get away from the law. I wouldn't stay on the highway. I'd go to the dirt, where I knew how to manipulate the turns better'n they did. The revenuers never did have the cars, or the drivers, to catch up with the bootleggers."

Johnson and his bootlegging brothers, Fred and L. P., would drop off their off souped-up Fords at Berl Eddleman's North Carolina auto shop—with the license plates removed, to protect their anonymity—to have them fine-tuned. When the work was done, they'd pick the cars up and disappear into the night.

"Bootleggin', that was big business back then," recalled Johnson. "I was just interested in goin' fast and haulin' whiskey. My neck of the area, and over in Virginia, that's where the roots of the sport are. About all your good dirt-track drivers were involved in moonshine. That's kind of the way it started."

Junior Johnson was 16 when he entered his first race. He was plowing a field one day, walking barefoot behind the family mule, when one of his brothers pulled up in one of the family's famed whiskey cars bearing the news that the local race track was planning a race among area bootleggers.

"I tied my mule to the fence post where I was plowing at," Johnson recalled, "and I said, 'We gotta stop at the house so I can fetch me some shoes.'" Freshly shod, 16-year-old Junior Johnson finished second among all the grown men entered in the race.

In 1955, at the age of 24, Junior Johnson arrived home from a race to discover that the fire under his daddy's still had gone out. When Johnson relit the fire, as he done so many, many times before, revenue agents rushed out of the nearby woods and arrested him. Johnson was sentenced to two years in a federal penitentiary. By the time he was paroled after serving eleven months, he had become something of a folk hero in the stock car-happy south.

"I was probably the popularest person in the sport at that time," Johnson immodestly admitted. "I think the exposure of being a good moonshiner and having the fastest car of anybody, it was sort of a glorified thing, like Babe Ruth hitting his 714th home run."

Johnson's entire family was arrested on moonshining charges in 1958. His brothers, Fred and L. P., went to prison, where their father was already serving time. Their mother was fined and given a suspended sentence. But Junior himself beat the rap when NASCAR officials confirmed Johnson's alibi that he had been racing when the alleged offenses occurred.

NASCAR moved "uptown" in 1972 after the R. J. Reynolds tobacco company began pumping millions into the sport. Ironically, moonshiner Junior Johnson played a key role in ushering in the modern, mainstream, Madison Avenue era of stock car racing. Johnson was searching for $800,000 to further fund his already highly successful race team when he received word that the tobacco giant, which had recently been prohibited from advertising its cigarettes on TV and radio, was looking for new ways to promote its products. When Johnson learned that R. J. Reynolds was willing to spend much, much more money than he needed, he alertly put the tobacco company in touch with NASCAR czar Bill France.

Never again would NASCAR be simply a small clique of drivers and mechanics and their Southern race fans. To accommodate its new big-bucks backer, NASCAR changed the name of its Grand National series to Winston Cup. All races under 250 miles, once a staple of the circuit, were dropped from the schedule, as were all dirt surfaces and 13 short tracks. The schedule was reduced from 46 to 31 races. And, as some students of NASCAR politics hasten to point out, two of Johnson's drivers—Cale Yarborough and Darrell Waltrip—soon won six Winston Cup Championships between 1976 and 1985.

Junior Johnson won 50 Winston Cup races as a driver and 139 as a race team owner.

In 1985, Johnson, who as a convicted felon could not vote, get a passport or legally own a gun, was granted a full pardon by President Ronald Reagan. When John F. Kennedy was elected president in 1960, Johnson had wryly noted: "His daddy was a bootlegger, and he went to the White House. My daddy was a bootlegger, and both of us went to federal prison."

Fireball Roberts

Soft-spoken Daytona Beach hometown hero Edward Glenn "Fireball" Roberts—who earned his nickname as a hard-throwing high school baseball pitcher, not because of any fiery crashes—was NASCAR's first superstar. Roberts rejected offers of college scholarships and minor-league baseball contracts to pursue his first love: driving fast cars. But until Roberts won the 1962 Daytona 500, he had felt jinxed at his hometown track.

"I just didn't know if I would make it," admitted Roberts, who was knocked out by a busted fuel pump and two blown engines in the first three 500s. "It's like a dream come true. I can't really believe it's happened."

"He has just driven his cotton-pickin' heart out on this track trying to win the big one," his wife, Doris, declared.

Roberts, who made a habit of driving his cars into the ground, knew no other way to race. So, understandably, he detested the new Daytona International Speedway phenomenon known as "the draft." It galled Roberts that in 1962 a

Glenn "Fireball" Roberts, of Daytona Beach, holds his trophy after winning the first Firecracker 250 stock car race in Daytona Beach, Fla., July 4, 1959. Roberts won with an average speed of 140.581 miles per hour in a 1959 Pontiac, and received $4,100. (AP Photo)

driver like young Richard Petty could keep his clearly out-classed car in contention by clinging to the bumper of Roberts's car lap after lap. Finally, Roberts broke free, finishing 27 seconds in front.

Although Roberts, who regularly dined on bologna-and-cheese sandwiches, had begun racing on the beach course in 1947, his only previous victory in his hometown of Daytona had occurred in a 1955 Grand National race. And that one was wiped off the books when a postrace inspection revealed the push rods in Roberts's engine had been altered.

"The only big race I ever won in Daytona was on the beach, and they took that one away from me," muttered Roberts.

Fireball had moved all the way up from 46th place to the lead in the 1959 Daytona inaugural, only to have his fuel pump break.

In 1960, Roberts, piloting a new Pontiac that had been prepped by Daytona Beach garage owner Smokey Yunick, was the fastest qualifier with an eye-catching speed of 151.556 mph. At the time, that was faster than any open-wheel driver had ever gone at rival Indianapolis Motor Speedway—a fact that image-conscious Daytona officials were happy to publicize.

Fireball was the pole winner in 1961, reaching 155.709 mph, and again in '62, when he was clocked at 156.999 mph. In fact, beginning with Cotton Owens's 143.198 mph in the 1959 inaugural, the top qualifying speed at Daytona increased each year except 1965 until Cale Yarborough reached 194.015 mph in 1970.

Comfortably in front with 13 laps to go in 1961, Roberts was contemplating victory when the engine in his black and gold Pontiac blew up.

He watched in dejected silence as former mechanic Marvin Panch, driving Roberts's discarded 1960 Pontiac, rolled to victory.

"I can't win here," Roberts groaned. "I just can't win a big one here. What the hell's with this town that I can't win here?"

Despite some earlier success on the NASCAR Grand National circuit, Marvin Panch admittedly was almost broke in 1961 when he got his big break at Roberts's expense. Panch used his $21,050 first prize to buy a home in Daytona.

Fireball Roberts was critically injured in a fiery crash in Charlotte, N.C., in May, 1964. It was his close friend and fellow driver Ned Jarrett who pulled Fireball's charred body out of the burning car, while Roberts cried, "Help me, Ned. I'm burning up."

Roberts lay in a hospital bed, in great pain, for two months. Infection set in, but Fireball never lost his sense of humor. While attendants washed away the gangrene, Roberts would refer to himself as "The Jolly Green Giant." To pass the time, Roberts would sing Faron Young's "Hello, Walls" over and over at the top of his lungs.

Finally a doctor warned him, "If you don't settle down and behave yourself, you're gonna die."

"If I'd ever worried about that," Roberts shot back, "I wouldn't be here in the first place."

On July 2, 1964, Fireball Roberts died. And the racing world grieved as it would not grieve again until the tragic death of Dale Earnhardt in 2001. Roberts was buried a mile from Daytona International Speedway.

Tiny Lund

DeWayne L. "Tiny" Lund—so known because of his nearly 300 pounds—traveled to Daytona in February of 1963, hoping to land a job helping out on somebody's pit crew. Lund didn't particularly care whose race team, or doing what. He just wanted to be a part of the big show. According to legend, Lund had 18 cents in his pocket when he hit town.

A former high school football and basketball star back home in his native Iowa, the 26-year-old Tiny Lund ran a fishing camp in South Carolina and enjoyed racing motorcycles in addition to stock cars. But in 131 tries on the Grand National circuit, he had never won a race. He had begun to believe that he never would.

On Feb. 14, 1963, when 1961 Daytona 500 winner Marvin Panch lost control of his Maserati and crashed during testing for the 250-mile American Challenge Cup sports car race at Daytona International Speedway, Tiny Lund was one of the first on the scene. Panch's car, which had struck the guard rail and cartwheeled down the track, was upside down

Tiny Lund of Cross, S.C., waits at the Daytona International Speedway for the arrival of his all-new 1969 Camaro on July 3, 1970. Lund raced in the Paul Revere 250 NASCAR Grand American Series race which started at midnight July 4, 1970. (AP Photo)

on its roof and on fire when Lund, who just happened to be nearby, rushed to the wreck. Inside, Panch was frantically trying to escape, but the car door wouldn't open.

"I was kicking and trying to get out and I couldn't," Panch later recalled. "No way. There wasn't a hole big enough to crawl through."

In addition to battling the blaze with a fire extinguisher, Lund used his size and his strength to help lift the car far enough off the ground to allow Panch to push the door partially open. Then Lund grabbed Panch's ankle and pulled his seriously burned fellow driver to safety.

"When the gas tank blew . . . everything bad I did in my life flashed before me like I was watching a TV screen," Panch admitted. "All in a matter of a split second, but it seemed like an hour."

For their efforts, Lund and four rescuers received Carnegie Medals for heroism. And Lund was quickly selected to replace Panch as the driver of the Wood Brothers Ford in the upcoming Daytona 500.

Taking full advantage of swift, efficient pit stops and a shrewd fuel strategy, Tiny Lund—who ran out of gas in the fourth and final turn—literally coasted across the finish line in first place after Fred Lorenzen and Ned Jarrett, the only other drivers on the lead lap, both had to stop for fuel. In Victory Lane, Lund let out a loud hog call and announced he would invest his $24,550 in winnings in his backwoods fishing camp.

In 1963, Big Bill France had promised a $10,000 bonus to the first driver to top 180 mph at his new track. That was why Marvin Panch had been so willing to test the new Maserati.

"They were looking for a dummy to try it out," he later explained. "And I was eager. I figured, 'I can knock this off.'"

The 1963 Daytona 500 was also the first race covered by ABC's *Wide World of Sports*, the two-year-old TV show that specialized in tape-delayed broadcasts of obscure and usual sports events. ABC's coverage of the 1963 Daytona 500 didn't actually air until three weeks later, when it was presented along with a report on dog sled racing in New Hampshire. Nevertheless, it marked the dawn of a new era for Daytona and for NASCAR.

The United States Auto Club lifted its ban in 1963 and allowed its drivers to compete in the Daytona 500 for the first time. As a result, open-wheel stars A. J. Foyt, Johnny Ruther-ford, Rodger Ward, Parnelli Jones, Jim Hurtubise and Troy Ruttman all traveled to Daytona. Rutherford fared the best, winning one of the two qualifying races and eventually finish-ing ninth.

Tiny Lund's wife, Wanda, had once dated stock car driver LeeRoy Yarbrough. So it probably should have come as no surprise that, although the two men were friends—Lund, a gentle, fun-loving giant, and the nasty-tempered Yarbrough, who later won the 1969 Daytona 500—they frequently feuded.

According to Wanda, the first time she met Lund, Tiny "turned me over his knee and set my heinie-end on fire like a two-year-old kid. We were an item after that."

When Tiny Lund and Wanda first started dating, he took her to Daytona. Perched atop Lund's truck in the infield to get a better view of the track, Wanda soon lay down and fell asleep. When Tiny returned after qualifying for the 500, he proudly asked, "Well, what did you think?"

"I went to sleep," Wanda said.

"You went to sleep!" Lund exclaimed. "For God's sake, why?"

"It took you too long to come around," Wanda explained.

"Hell," Tiny barked back, "I was going 180 miles an hour!"

One year at Daytona, as a practical joke, Tiny Lund hid a pair of his wife's panties in rival driver Bobby Unser's suit-case, hoping Unser's own wife would find them when Bobby returned home.

But Unser evened the score at Daytona the next spring. Unser talked a hotel desk clerk into giving him a key to Lund's room, then filled all of Tiny's pockets and all of his shoes with shaving cream.

Buddy Baker

No driver ever wanted the win the Daytona 500 more than Buddy Baker, who began his quest in 1961 at the tender age of 21. And no driver ever experienced more anguish trying to get that coveted checkered flag. Four times during the 1970s, Buddy Baker found himself staring at a possible victory in the Daytona 500. And four times he went home heartbroken and empty-handed.

Teammate and boyhood friend Richard Petty beat Baker in 1971, when Buddy was snookered in the pits. Two years later, Baker won the pole and led for 157 laps before blowing his engine with six laps to go. In 1975, he was out in front by half a lap when his motor quit.

In '76, Baker was again leading the Daytona 500 when his engine simply stopped. He hurriedly called in to crew chief Harry Hyde. "Harry," Baker said, "This thing just quit."

"Buddy Baker, you better be telling a lie," Hyde replied.

Buddy Baker, of Charlotte, NC, holds a trophy presented to him after he won the pole position on February 9, 1969, for the Daytona 500 Grand National stock car race with a one-lap speed of 188.901 miles per hour in his 1969 Dodge Charger. (AP Photo)

"Do you hear anything?" Buddy shot back.

And the engine, of course, was quiet.

By the time Baker coasted into his pit, his entire crew, frustrated by their driver's string of calamities at Daytona, had gone back to the garage to begin packing for the depressing trip home.

In 1977, Buddy Baker finished third at Daytona behind Cale Yarborough.

After another blown engine cost him a chance at victory in 1978, when he held the lead with five laps to go, Baker asked, "What has a fellow got to do?"

In 1979, Baker, who knew only one way to race—wide open—again sat on the pole at Daytona. He was brimming with confidence when his car began sputtering on the first lap.

Finally, in 1980, driving a silver and black Oldsmobile that rivals respectfully referred to as "The Grey Ghost," Baker was able to put 500 miles together without a mishap and claim the coveted checkered flag.

Unlike 1971, in 1980 it was the competition that was outsmarted on the final pit stops, with 20 laps to go. Neil Bonnett's stop for gas consumed 11 seconds. Bobby Allison, who opted for two new tires, was stopped even longer. Dale Earnhardt, who appeared to pose the stiffest threat, had to make a second emergency stop after his tire changer neglected to tighten the lug nuts.

Meanwhile, Buddy Baker, who paused only long enough to take on an 11-gallon can of gas, was in and out of his pit in six seconds, never to be caught again.

Worried that misfortune might strike yet again and Baker might run out of gas, crew chief Waddell Wilson urged Buddy to ease off the throttle a bit during the closing laps.

"I'm not stopping!" Baker shouted over the radio.

This time it was Baker's turn to catch a break as the final three laps of the race were run under the caution flag after a blown engine spewed oil on the track. Despite the late yellow, Baker averaged 177.602 mph—a Daytona record.

"When I won, oh man, that was it," Baker declared. "To me, the world was lifted off my shoulders. There was nowhere to go from there. To me, that was my lifetime goal. And once I got there, I really didn't know how to react. I had waited so long it was almost a shock to me that things went as well as they did.

"The thing about Daytona, it's really a measure of your career," Baker continued. "No matter what, I had won the Daytona 500. That registers more than names or records or anything else. It's something you're remembered for."

Buddy's father, Buck Baker, was a NASCAR driver of considerable renown in his own right. Buck Baker won the drivers' championship in 1956 and '57.

Baker's given name was Elzie Wylie. No wonder he preferred to be called Buddy.

Someone once asked Buddy Baker how many times he had won the Daytona 500?

"Once," he replied. "But I won the Daytona 475 eleven times."

Mario and A.J.

They said Mario Andretti was too short to drive a stock car. They scoffed at his racing style, which included diving to the bottom of the banking during the turns instead of staying as wide as possible.

Incredibly, even some members of Andretti's own Holman-Moody race team seemed intent upon undermining Mario's chances in the 1967 Daytona 500. When Andretti complained about his lack of speed during practice sessions, his crew chief, Jake Elder, admitted team owner John Holman had equipped Mario with an engine with medium risers instead of the high risers that he had given to Mario's teammate, 1965 Daytona 500 winner Fred Lorenzen. Andretti had to carry his protest all the way to the chief of Ford motor sports, Jacque Passino, to get that injustice rectified.

During the 500, when Andretti and Lorenzen, the only two drivers on the lead lap, pulled into their respective pits for their final stops under a caution flag, Andretti became convinced his jack man purposely held his car in the air until after

Mario Andretti, left, of Nazareth, Pa., and Jackie Ickx, Brussels, Belgium give a victory sign after they won the Six-Hour Daytona Continental driving a Ferrari 312/P at the Daytona International Speedway. The race took place atDaytona Beach, Fla., on Sunday, Feb. 6, 1972. (AP Photo)

Lorenzen had returned to the track. In spite of all that, Andretti passed Lorenzen on the restart and won going away.

From there, Andretti, who for years had to hide the fact that he was racing at all from his immigrant father, went on to win the 1969 Indianapolis 500 and the 1978 Formula One World Driving Championship.

Andretti was so small that the seat in his car had to be modified to accommodate him.

"The chair is like a baby chair," explained car co-owner Ralph Moody. "He's so short, the pedal and throttle had to be built up."

A. J. Foyt, already an American racing icon with three Indianapolis 500 victories to his credit, boldly predicted he

A.J. Foyt, of Houston, Tex., takes a look at the trophy he won for finishing first in the Firecracker 400 stock car race at Daytona Beach, Fla., July 4, 1964. Foyt was the winner of the Indianapolis 500 race earlier this year. (AP Photo)

would win the 1972 Daytona 500. Then he backed it up by posting one of the fastest average speeds (161.550 mph) and one of the largest winning margins (nearly two laps) in Daytona 500 history.

"I had to run harder to keep my word," A. J. joked afterwards. "It's been a dream of mine since I got into stock car racing. I've won at Indy three times and I've won at Le Mans. I've always wanted to win the Daytona 500 because I feel this is the greatest stock car race in the world."

Sterling Marlin

On his way to Daytona International Speedway, early on the morning of the 1994 Daytona 500, Sterling Marlin stopped at a fast-food restaurant for a quick breakfast. He was 0-for-278 at that point in his Winston Cup career. Marlin craved a predawn hamburger, but the weary waitress on duty grumbled that it was too early, so Sterling settled for a couple of sausage-and-egg sandwiches. Later that day, Marlin—who had qualified fourth, drove car No. 4, and was assigned space number four on pit road—became the fifth driver to collect his first career win in the biggest of all stock car races, the Daytona 500.

Naturally, on his way to the track on race day the following year, defending Daytona 500 champion Sterling Marlin stopped at that same joint and ordered two more of those sausage-and-egg sandwiches. Marlin was even more dominant in the 500 in 1995, leading 105 of the 200 laps and holding off Dale Earnhardt at the finish.

Sterling Marlin of Columbia, Tenn., sprays champagne in Victory Lane after winning his second Daytona 500 Sunday February 19, 1995, at Daytona International Speedway. (AP Photo/Terry Renna)

In 1994, as Marlin pulled away from runner-up Ernie Irvan, Terry Labonte, and Jeff Gordon, with his heart pounding, he kept telling himself, "It's just like a thirty-lap Saturday night feature at Nashville."

But he wasn't kidding anyone, including himself.

"This is the Daytona 500," growled Earnhardt, who by that time was 0-for-17 on the big oval and obviously counting. "I ain't supposed to win the damn thing."

Marlin, whose race driver father, Coo Coo, Marlin went winless throughout his sixteen-year Winston Cup career, now had two Daytona 500 victories to his credit—his only two Winston Cup wins.

"I just wish everybody could sit in that seat and feel the feeling to win this thing," Marlin said. "It sends cold chills all over you."

Sterling Marlin's victory in 1994 was marred by the deaths of two drivers—popular veteran Neil Bonnett and rookie Rodney Orr—who were killed in separate crashes while practicing during Speed Weeks.

"You just wonder, why? Why this race?" said Dale Earnhardt of his close friend, Bonnett, a veteran of 14 Daytona 500s. "But that is the side of racing that is there. I live with it. I understand it. I have no problem with it."

In 2001, deeply saddened and understandably shaken by the death of Dale Earnhardt, Sterling Marlin flew home to Tennessee immediately after the race. He was watching the 11 o'clock TV news when he heard the announcer say that he, Marlin, had delivered "a vicious tap" that caused NASCAR legend Earnhardt to crash.

The next morning, Marlin's office received death threats—not only against Sterling but against his family and members of his race team as well. More ugly threats arrived in the mail. Marlin's web site was inundated with angry e-mail. The likeable, easy-going Sterling was stunned.

"I knew we didn't do nothing wrong," he said. "It was totally a racin' deal. There was nothing we could do about it. If the seat belt hadn't broke, Dale would be here today."

Both Dale Earnhardt Jr. and race winner Michael Waltrip jumped to Marlin's defense.

"I didn't see it [the fatal crash] being anybody's fault," said Waltrip, who caught a glimpse of the crash in his rearview mirror as he raced toward the finish line for the long-awaited first victory of his 17-year career.

The whole incident was so painful that Marlin still prefers not to talk about it.

A spin by Robby Gordon with nine laps remaining in the 2002 Daytona 500 probably cost race leader Jeff Gordon his third 500 victory. "I hated to see that caution come out," Gordon lamented later. "We were in perfect position."

On the restart, with five laps to go, Sterling Marlin tried to pass Jeff Gordon on the inside. When Gordon moved down to block him, the two cars collided. The left side of Marlin's car dipped below the yellow line—a violation of NASCAR's rules—but Gordon spun, allowing Sterling to grab the lead.

"Me being spun was my fault," Gordon admitted afterward. "[Marlin] had a run on me on the restart and I had to get down to block him. I got myself spun. I messed up both of our days."

"If I was in his shoes, I would have tried to block me, too," Marlin conceded.

Of course, at that point in the race, Marlin could afford to be gracious. He had the lead. And the checkered flag was waiting.

But as every stock car fan knows, in NASCAR things are not always as they appear.

After the cars were red-flagged to a halt on the backstretch because of a five-car pile-up that had occurred at the starting line, behind the leaders, Marlin—who was parked in perfect position, directly behind the pace car—climbed out the window of his car to see how much damage had been done to his right fender in the collision with Gordon. Realizing that his crumpled fender was rubbing against his tire, Marlin gave the sheet metal a yank.

"I seen [Dale] Earnhardt get out and clean off his windshield [during a red-flag stop] at Richmond in 1987, so I thought it was okay," Marlin explained, somewhat sheepishly. "I guess maybe it wasn't. NASCAR didn't like it. We was damned if we did and damned if we didn't. I was just trying to call NASCAR's bluff. What were they going to do to me, throw me in jail?"

After a lengthy, animated debate, NASCAR's brass decided to ignore Marlin's foray below the yellow line. "[Gordon] run me down below it," Marlin explained.

But when the race was resumed nineteen minutes later, NASCAR ordered Sterling to the back of the pack for working on his car during the red-flag timeout. That put Ward Burton out in front by default. And that was where the No. 22 car stayed for the final two laps, finishing just ahead of Elliott Sadler and Geoffrey Bodine, who almost died in a truck race at Daytona two years earlier.

"When the 40 car [Marlin] had to go to the end of the longest line, that put us in the hot seat," Burton said. "But I might have done the same thing in the same scenario. We all make mistakes in the heat of the moment."

23

O for Daytona

Few drivers have felt more frustration at Daytona than Rusty Wallace. "Every time we leave the place in February, we know that it's a full year until we'll get another shot at winning the thing," he admitted. But Wallace refuses to give up hope.

"We definitely know what great drivers like Darrell Waltrip and Dale Earnhardt went through before they won it, and I'll guarantee you there'll be a hell of a celebration when we pull it off," said Wallace, whose first Daytona 500 start came back in 1982.

"I love Daytona. It's breathtaking. I used to sit in the grandstands with my pop and watch it. I used to get on the fence and watch them come blowing by, and they would blow your hair straight up in the air from all the breeze. I never thought I'd be racing here.

"It would be a great day in my career to take that checkered flag, that's for sure."

Veteran NASCAR driver Rusty Wallace is helped into the driver's seat by mechanic Rob Jones at Daytona International Speedway in Daytona Beach, Fla., Friday, Feb. 15, 2002. (AP Photo/Peter Cosgrove)

In 1983, Rusty Wallace crashed in the backstretch, trying to qualify for the Daytona 500. He wrecked again in the 1984 race. Beginning in 1991, Rusty crashed at Daytona for five years in a row.

Wallace was feeling pretty good about himself with about 30 laps remaining in the 1993 Daytona 500 when another car rammed him.

In 1998, Rusty had led or been up among the leaders most of the afternoon before he was forced to settle for fifth place behind Dale Earnhardt.

After leading more than half of the 500 in 1999, Wallace let Jeff Gordon slip past him with 10 laps to go. When Gordon drove down under Wallace on the apron, Rusty had to make an instant decision. He could move up on the track to give Gordon room, compromising his own position, or he could let Jeff crash into Ricky Rudd, whose damaged car was dead ahead, desperately trying to get up to speed. Much to his subsequent regret, Rusty—who had been known to be reckless over the years—elected to be courteous this time.

"I said, 'Man, I'm not going to wreck a bunch of cars,'" Wallace explained later.

"It felt like I was coming up on [Rudd] at a thousand miles an hour," Gordon admitted. "I was getting ready to hold on tight. I was going to have to get on my brake real hard, or—I don't know what else could have happened."

As soon as Wallace gave Gordon room, Jeff blew by him, taking a long line of cars with him. Wallace eventually ended up eighth.

"To tell you the truth, that should have been me sitting over there in Victory Lane," Wallace groaned as Gordon celebrated. "You talk about the most sick feeling. I pulled the car into the garage and I looked myself in the eye and I said, 'Self, what just happened in the last three minutes? You led that damn race all day long!'"

Mark Martin is another driver who, try as he might, has not met with much success at Daytona.

"You don't ask people who haven't won any races ever when they are going to win the Daytona 500," Martin pointed out, trying to put a positive spin on his predicament. "So I guess it's an honor, sort of."

Martin knows what he's talking about. Back in the early 1980s, he nearly went broke trying to win a race.

"I had nothing," he recalled. "I had to auction off all my stuff. Financially and emotionally, I had to start all over again. But I wouldn't change a thing. I wouldn't be the same person if I did."

Mark Martin underwent spinal fusion surgery following the end of the 1999 NASCAR season. He finished fourth in the final race of the year on Nov. 21 in Atlanta, flew home to Florida that night and was operated on the next morning.

"I left the house at 5:30 a.m.," he recounted. "I checked into the hospital and by 7 a.m. I was under the knife. I was back in my room before I realized what had been done."

For two years, Martin had lived with excruciating pain caused by the bulging degenerated disk in his lower back. Sitting for three hours in a souped-up automobile, hurtling around race tracks in bone-jarring circles at 180 mph, didn't do anything to ease his agony.

"I only hurt when I moved," Martin admitted with a grin.

Doctors removed the damaged bone and inserted additional bone and supporting hardware to fuse and stabilize Martin's lower back.

Mark Martin, from Batesville, Ark., stands on top of his Ford after winning the Bud Shootout Sunday, Feb. 7, 1999, at the Daytona international Speedway in Daytona Beach, Fla. (AP Photo/Tony Gutierrez)

When Martin awoke after surgery, the nurse on duty asked if he would like to try to sit up for a minute. Instead, Martin stood up and walked to the door of his room and back.

"The next day, I walked down the hall," he said. On the third day, Martin discarded his walker.

"I'm a compulsive person—I don't ever just dabble in anything," Martin explained. "My goal was to be bullet-proof by the Daytona 500."

For the next six weeks, Martin was forced to lie flat on his back, staring at the ceiling, 22 hours out of each day. No TV, no telephone, no nothing. The other two hours were spent in physical therapy. On Jan. 21, a mere two months after his surgery, Martin was back at Daytona for a 32-lap test run.

"The doctors just stood there with their mouths open," Martin said. "They couldn't believe it."

A month later, three months after major surgery, Martin finished a remarkable fifth in the 2000 Daytona 500 behind Dale Jarrett.

"I'm just a hillbilly from Arkansas," Mark Martin once acknowledged. "This is the American dream. This is what every kid wants to do. I've made it a lot further than I ever expected.

"I never knew I was good enough to race against Richard Petty. And beat him. I never knew I could win all the Winston Cup races I've won. A lot of people would like to trade places with me."

Rusty Wallace was a wide-eyed 11-year-old youngster when Dave Marcis made his NASCAR Winston Cup debut at Daytona International Speedway in 1968—wearing wing-tipped shoes. That was three years before Jeff Gordon was born.

"I remember when I came out of the tunnel for the first time at Daytona," said Marcis. "I looked around and I couldn't believe the size of the place. And the mystique of the track is amazing."

Marcis, still wearing his wing-tips, retired from Winston Cup in 2002 after running in his 33rd Daytona 500 at the age of 60.

When Marcis decided in 1968 that he needed to move from the Wisconsin short-track circuit to NASCAR hotbed North Carolina in order to pursue his stock car career, he borrowed a friend's truck, hitched it to the mobile home in which he and his wife, Helen, were living, and personally pulled their house trailer 1,000 miles, halfway across the country.

"You find out right away that you have to have permits to pull those things," Marcis recalled. "I probably got about 12 miles down the road and got stopped. The rest of the way, Helen drove ahead in our Camaro and got the permits in each state. What a guy won't do to go racing."

Dave Marcis was typical of the independent jack-of-all-trades drivers upon whom NASCAR was built—guys like Frank Warren, D. K. Ulrich, and James Hilton. However, for the last 20 years of his racing career, Marcis increasingly became an anachronism, the last of a vanishing breed. No high-tech, state-of-the-art equipment for Dave. No luxurious motor home. No private jet. None of the creature comforts so common in modern-day Winston Cup. Marcis and his wife traveled from race to race in their van. Over the years, more than one all-you-can-eat restaurant along the way ordered Marcis, a voracious eater, never to set foot in their buffet line again. Often, Marcis survived on bologna sandwiches, sleeping in the cab of his truck.

In 1978, Dave Marcis's employer, Osterlund Racing, brought a rookie driver to Atlanta for a one-race audition. Although Marcis had already given notice that he would be quitting at the end of the season because of a spat with the team manager, he resented the presence of the upstart rookie and intentionally bumped into the side of the kid's car during the race. The brash rookie immediately bumped Marcis back. The rookie's name was Dale Earnhardt. The next season, Osterlund hired Earnhardt to replace Marcis.

Helen Marcis wanted a nice new house, a home the couple could call their own. But, as Dave recalled, "I convinced her that we needed to build a [race] shop before a house if I was ever going to get a sponsor. We had to have some equity to show a sponsor that we had some equipment and a place."

Veteran driver Dave Marcis is shown in his Arden, N.C. shop, Friday, March 30, 2001. Marcis has been without a big-bucks deal for nearly his entire career. During his most competitive period, in the late 1970s, he drove for owners with deep pockets and got four of his five victories. (AP Photo/Alan Marler)

As a result, the couple lived in their trailer for more than 20 years. The shop opened in 1987. Helen Marcis didn't get her new house until 1990.

"A lot of guys just drive," Marcis explained. "I work on the car. I drive the transporter. I do whatever needs to be done."

At the end, some said the sport had passed Marcis by. Winner of just five races in 882 tries, he hadn't finished in the top five since 1987.

Dale Earnhardt Jr. was a one-year-old wearing diapers when Marcis won his 125-mile qualifying heat at Daytona in 1976. Tony Stewart was four years old when Marcis finished second behind Richard Petty in the 1975 Winston Cup points race. Marcis's 33 appearances in the Daytona 500 broke a record set by the King himself. Petty is also the only driver ever to start more Cup races (1,177) than Marcis (882). Still, Marcis retired reluctantly.

"I still think I'm a qualified race car driver," said Marcis, who won for the last time at Richmond in 1982. "We just don't have the resources to run like the rest of the circuit. The sport is getting so costly that a small team can't keep up."

As multicar teams and multimillion-dollar budgets became commonplace, Dave Marcis remained a throwback who wore leather-soled, wing-tip shoes and saved his used spark plugs. He was an independent owner/driver who operated without the support and trappings of a deep-pocketed corporate sponsor. By the time he retired in 2002, Marcis had been the only independent operating on NASCAR's No. 1 circuit since J. D. McDuffie was killed in a crash at Watkins Glen in 1991.

"I guess I didn't keep up with the growth," Marcis admitted. "As an independent, working on my own car and driving it, I was too busy for anything else. I guess I didn't pay attention sometimes to what was going on around me."

In the end, Marcis blew an engine and had to be pushed off the track on the 80th lap of his final Daytona 500 in 2002 after a piece of paper stuck to the front end of his Chevrolet. Marcis's crew removed the paper during a pit stop, but the damage had been done.

"After it'd been that hot, the engine didn't run right. The water temperature went up to 260 degrees and the engine just wouldn't run right," Marcis explained. "You can't run 'em at 260 degrees."

Up and coming NASCAR star Tony Stewart suffers from claustrophobia—which can pose a problem when you make your living piloting hot, cramped race cars.

"When it gets hot, when the air I'm breathing gets hot, that's when it really gets to me," Stewart explained before the 2001 Daytona 500. "That's when I want to get out of the car." Unfortunately, Stewart's car is usually traveling 190 miles an hour in heavy traffic at the time.

He can feel it every time he climbs through the window into the front seat of his car. The gnawing, nervous feeling in his stomach. The sweat on his palms and his forehead and inside his fire suit. The fear. The panic. The urge to escape. Sometimes even breathing becomes a chore. The roof over his head, the two doors that don't open, the dashboard—they all seem so close. At times they all seem to be closing in. It gets worse the moment Stewart pulls on his helmet and straps on his safety harness and head-and-neck support system. And when the race starts and the engine heats up, and the temperature inside his orange Pontiac Grand Prix begins to climb, that's when Stewart really begins to sweat.

NASCAR driver Tony Stewart lifts the trophy after winning the Budweiser Shootout Sunday, Feb. 11, 2001, at the Daytona International Speedway in Daytona Beach, Fla. (AP Photo/Terry Renna)

Sometimes Stewart's crew chief, Greg Zipadelli, has to get on the radio and try to talk Tony through the remaining laps until the next pit stop. Sometimes his crew dumps a bag of ice cubes into the car's cooling system. "A dollar-fifty bag of ice, that usually will save me in a pinch," Stewart said. "I try to picture the air conditioner at home in my car. That usually makes me feel better. As long as I'm breathing cool air, it isn't so bad." It has been that way Stewart's entire life. And he doesn't know why.

"It's not like my sister held me under the blanket when I was little, nothing like that," he said. "But I never did like being in small, cramped places.

"I didn't notice it when I started racing go-karts because I wasn't strapped in," Stewart continued. "And it wasn't so bad in Indy cars, because there wasn't a roof over my head. It was tighter but it was more open. But when I got into stock cars [in 1999], I started to feel closed in."

Yet Stewart has never tried to get professional help. "When would I have time?" he snapped, in typical Tony Stewart smart-aleck fashion. "I barely have time to eat lunch."

Tony Stewart's sharp tongue has made him a villain to many NASCAR fans.

"When you become a competitive driver in Winston Cup racing, you're going to have a group of people who like you for what you do—and a group of people who don't like you," he explained with a shrug.

"It happened to Darrell Waltrip. It happened to Dale Earnhardt. It happened to Jeff Gordon. It happened to the best guys in the sport. To be in that group is kind of an honor. You know you're important enough for them to make the effort to boo you.

"If I was always relaxed and having fun and joking with the fans, I bet I wouldn't be a very good race car driver," Stewart said. "You've got to remember that we race 38 weekends. We're with each other 38 weekends a year. It's like a big, giant family. You've got so many people involved that eventually you're going to disagree with somebody along the line. It's like the Waltons on steroids."

When Stewart showed up at Daytona in 2002, he announced he was turning over a new leaf.

"I've drawn a line in saying what my obligations are," announced the new kinder, gentler, calmer Stewart. "My obligation is to drive that race car, put on a good show for the fans, and do the best job that I can for Joe Gibbs Racing. My contract is with Joe Gibbs Racing and nobody else.

"There are some people that we know that we can't trust," Stewart said, "and we're just not talking with those people this year.

"I'm not a bad guy," he insisted. "I just want to win and do my job."

There is a softer side to Tony Stewart, too. He plays Monopoly and ping-pong. He enjoys vintage cars and video games. He owns a kennel of greyhounds and cares so much about his dogs that, whenever one of the animals retires from racing and is adopted, Stewart flies that dog to his new home in his personal eight-passenger Citation Bravo jet.

"They sit in the same plane that I sit in," Stewart said. "They're racers, too. They're good enough to ride in my plane."

Rookies

Once, the yellow strip of tape that NASCAR places on the rear bumper of every rookie's car was considered a stigma. Today it is a badge of honor. Being young is no longer a bad thing.

"There's a different curve today," noted stock car king Richard Petty, the winner of seven Winston Cup championships and seven Daytona 500s. "Used to be you had to work your way up. Now they just take 'em and cram 'em into a Cup car."

Dale Earnhardt had raced at Daytona International Speedway for 17 years before he finally got to sit on the pole at the start of the 1996 Daytona 500. Rookie Jimmie Johnson earned that honor in 2002—on his first try.

"I always wanted to come here and be successful," said Johnson, who drives a car owned by Rick Hendrick and Jeff

Kevin Harvick, left, congratulates Jimmie Johnson, right, after Johnson qualified for the pole position Saturday, Feb. 9, 2002, for the Daytona 500 in Daytona Beach, Fla. (AP Photo/Terry Renna)

Gordon. "But to come here and sit on the pole right away—I really haven't soaked it all in yet."

On Johnson's way to the track for the annual Thursday Twin 125s in 2002, cars filled with fans who recognized his suddenly famous 26-year-old face honked their horns or flashed him the thumbs-up sign.

"That kind of stuff never happened to me before," Johnson admitted.

At the team's souvenir trailer, caps and model cars bearing Johnson's No. 48 quickly sold out. "It's amazing how excited these fans have become overnight," Johnson said.

A TV camera crew knocked on the door of his grandmother's home in San Diego, requesting an interview, during the week. "She was scared to death," Johnson said. "She's never been on TV."

"I feel like I'm on the outside, looking in," Johnson admitted. "It's weird. This is wild. It's been a whole new adventure."

Admittedly baffled by the intricacies of the all-important draft at Daytona, the rookie pole sitter sought the advice of his team owner/boss/teammate/racing rival Jeff Gordon. Johnson went to Gordon's motor home four days before the 2002 Daytona 500, spread all of his credit cards out on the counter as if they were race cars in order to simulate various drafting situations, and then asked Gordon what he should do.

"How many Daytona 500s have you been in?" Gordon asked.

The answer, of course, was none.

"Well, stop worrying so much," Gordon urged. "Just go out there and learn."

Former Winston Cup champion Dale Jarrett was thirty-four years old when he won his first race after six years of trying. Rusty Wallace was twenty-nine, with 71 races under his belt, when he finally reached Victory Lane. Kevin Harvick got there in 2001—after two races.

Harvick was sitting at home in North Carolina, watching the race on TV when Dale Earnhardt hit the wall in the 2001 Daytona 500. Harvick was supposed to just get his feet wet in 2001. Instead, one race into the season, he was thrown head-first into the fray. In 2001, the twenty-five-year-old Harvick was supposed to keep his eyes open and his mouth shut. Instead, he was by far the busiest driver in NASCAR. Not only did Harvick win two Winston Cup races and Rookie of the Year honors—with the ghost of Dale Earnhardt in his rearview mirror—he also finished a surprising ninth in the driver points, won $4.3 million, and grabbed the Busch championship as well. Compare that to Jeff Gordon, Rusty Wallace, Dale Jarrett, and Bill Elliott—none of whom won even once during their freshman years in Winston Cup.

Running sixty-eight races, sleeping on airplanes and eating on pit road, sometimes crisscrossing the country on a weekend to compete full-time on both the Winston Cup and Busch circuits—something no other driver had ever done—Harvick lost 15 pounds. Somehow Kevin also found time to get married.

"When I look back on it, if things had gone really bad, it could have been the end of my career," Harvick admitted. "But I didn't have time to sit back and dwell on anything in depth. For the most part, everything was happening really fast. You've got to stop and pinch yourself when you think about everything we accomplished.

"I love to race—plain and simple," Harvick said. "Give me a bicycle, or a wagon for that matter, and I'll race it."

Rival drivers claim Kevin Harvick shares the late Dale Earnhardt's bump-and-run disposition on the race track. Many don't appreciate it—but it should come as no surprise. When he graduated from kindergarten, Harvick's parents gave him a go-kart as a gift. He immediately drove it into a fence. When Harvick was seven years old he spun his sister into the garage door as the two kids raced their Big Wheels.

"There will always be drivers who do things with their cars that everybody doesn't approve of, and there will always be people who are as smooth as silk," said Darrell Waltrip.

"He doesn't want to be Dale Earnhardt by any means," insisted crew chief Kevin Hamlin. "He wants to be his own person, and that's what we try to let him be. But as far as his driving style and what he wants to accomplish in a race car, you see some of the same characteristics. That's probably why Earnhardt liked him so well."

"I'm not Dale Earnhardt," Harvick insisted. "He was the greatest, and I'm just starting out."

In 2002, Shawna Robinson, a thirty-seven-year-old mother of two, became just the second woman to compete in the Daytona 500—and the first since Janet Guthrie in 1980. Guthrie also made the field for the 500 in 1977.

"I'm sure there are those drivers who think maybe I don't deserve to be here," Robinson admitted. "But I've worked harder to get here than some of them. I walk through this garage area with my head held high."

Unfortunately, Robinson ran out of gas at one point in the race and had to coast into the pits. She eventually ended up in 24th place.

"Women in sports have grown tremendously in the last few years," said Robinson. "What we need now is to see women winning."

Shawna Robinson waves to the crowd as she's introduced at Daytona International Speedway in Daytona Beach, Fla., Sunday, Feb. 17, 2002, for the Daytona 500. (AP Photo/Peter Cosgrove)

That's Racin'

Cape Canaveral, the center of attention in this country's ventures into outer space, is located just down the Florida coast from Daytona Beach. In an effort to capitalize on the country's new fascination with space exploration and travel during the early 1960s, the Air Force placed an Atlas missile booster rocket on display outside the fourth turn at Daytona in 1961.

The grandstands and towers at Daytona International Speedway pay homage to many of the heroes who have had the greatest impact on auto racing at Daytona Beach or in the annual 500. In addition to Richard Petty, Dale Earnhardt, Bobby and Davey Allison, Fireball Roberts, and Tiny Lund, there are sections of seating named for motor sports legends Barney Oldfield, Ralph DePalma, "Little Joe" Weatherly, Sir Malcolm Campbell, Sir Henry Segrave, Ray Keech, and Frank Lockhart.

Oldfield, whose name was synonymous with speed shortly after the turn of the last century, first came to Daytona in

1904 to race Alexander Winton's "Bullet 2" on the beach. He returned to Daytona in 1910 to set a world land speed record on the hard-packed sand.

DePalma, who won more than 2,000 races worldwide including the 1915 Indianapolis 500, broke the world land speed record on Daytona Beach in 1919. Many considered him to be the greatest American driver in the first quarter of the 20th century.

Weatherly, whose practical jokes made him racing's "Clown Prince," was a free-spirited star on the Southern dirt tracks and NASCAR's Modified circuit. Although Weatherly participated in only one Daytona 500, finishing fifth in the 1959 inaugural, he won the Winston Cup championships in 1962 and '63.

Nineteen-twenties dirt-track star Ray Keech joined the parade of record setters when he broke the world speed standard on Daytona Beach in 1928. The following year, Keech won the Indianapolis 500.

Engineer and driver Frank Lockhart, hailed as racing's "boy wonder" during the wide-open 1920s, won the 1926 Indy 500 as a rookie relief driver. Lockhart, who set speed records in nearly every race he entered, also designed the revolutionary Stutz "Blackhawk Special." He was killed at age 25 when his "Blackhawk Special" flipped during a 1928 attempt at a new world record on Daytona Beach.

The second Daytona 500 contrasted sharply to the accident-free inaugural the year before. Accidents and fires claimed 21 cars in 1960, so decimating the field that the next two races on the NASCAR schedule had to be canceled that season to give race teams an opportunity to rebuild and regroup.

A Chevy driven by Sgt. George Green, on leave from military service in Germany, suddenly burst into flames and slid nearly 300 yards before Green was able to bail out. Tommy Herbert's Ford flew apart after striking the fence on the backstretch, sending the engine 50 feet down the track and sending Herbert to the hospital.

When Tommy Irwin's '59 T-Bird plunged into Lake Lloyd in the middle of the infield as a result of a six-car pile-up on the backstretch during the 100-mile qualifying race, Irwin—still wearing his protective helmet—climbed out of his partially submerged car and swam to shore through water made choppy by a brisk wind. Fellow driver Tom Pistone was so shaken by the incident that he immediately had an air tank and emergency breathing device installed behind the driver's seat in his car. However, that apparatus was of little help when Pistone spun coming out of turn four on his final lap and slid backwards into two cars abandoned after an earlier wreck, breaking several ribs.

Early NASCAR star Fred Lorenzen, who had developed a reputation for winning big races, took advantage of Chrysler's one-year withdrawal from NASCAR as well as a driving rain which halted the race after 133 laps to win the 1965 Daytona 500.

"I just never thought I could do it," admitted Lorenzen, a driver from the Midwest who got his start in racing by winning a demolition derby at Chicago's Soldier Field. Ulcers forced Lorenzen to retire from racing when he was still in his prime.

   LeeRoy Yarbrough blew whatever chance he had to beat Cale Yarborough in the 1968 Daytona 500 when he misinterpreted a signal from his crew and unnecessarily pitted late in the race. But Yarbrough redeemed himself in 1969 when he overtook Charlie Glotzbach with a slingshot pass on the final turn—to the delight of more than 100,000 spectators, the largest crowd in Daytona history up until that time.

   "I just didn't know anything to do," a stunned Glotzbach admitted.

   "I just can't find words to express how exciting this is," an emotional Yarbrough declared. In Victory Lane after the race, LeeRoy Yarbrough exclaimed, "I'm going crazy!"

   Tragically, eleven years later, Yarbrough was committed to a psychiatric hospital after he tried to kill his own mother. The unthinkable incident occurred on the day of the 1980 Twin 125 qualifying races at Daytona. Minnie Yarbrough, who at the time was 80 years old, was brushing her hair when her son LeeRoy walked up behind her and put his hands on her shoulders.

   "I thought he was going to give me a hug," Minnie Yarbrough related later. "Then LeeRoy said, 'Mama, I hate to do this. Mama, I've got to kill you.'"

   A teenage nephew, hearing the struggle as Yarbrough tried to choke his mother, rushed into the room and slammed a quart jar full of preserves against LeeRoy's head, knocking the former driver out cold.

Yarbrough's bizarre conduct was later blamed on his heavy drinking and "lesions on the brain," possibly the result of the several serious car crashes that he had earlier been involved in. LeeRoy Yarbrough, winner of the stock car racing's biggest prize in 1969, died in a mental hospital in 1984.

Pete Hamilton, the son of a Harvard Ph.D.—hardly the sort of background that produced most of Daytona's early stars—won the 1970 Daytona 500 driving a distinctive, but short-lived, winged Petty Enterprises Plymouth SuperBird.

Early stock car star Bobby Isaac, who finished second in the Daytona 500 behind Richard Petty in 1973 and placed fifth in 1970, once hid in the infield after winning a race because he was afraid somebody might ask for his autograph. Isaac, who quit school as a teenager after his parents died in order to go to work in a sawmill, didn't want people to know that he couldn't read or write.

Personable former Detroit taxi cab driver and auto assembly-line worker Benny Parsons won only one Winston Cup race in 1975—and he only led four laps, including the final three, in that race. But that was enough to make Parsons the 1975 Daytona 500 champion. Parsons, the 1973 Winston Cup champion—even though he won only two races that year—had nearly quit racing after going winless in 1974. However, in 1975 he found himself in front of the field at Daytona with less than four laps to go when race leader David Pearson clipped the front end of Cale Yarborough's lapped car and spun out.

As a young man, Parsons had first visited Daytona International Speedway in 1963 as a fan. The sympathetic wife of driver H. B. Bailey slipped Parsons a pit pass "so I got to go over and watch 'em pump gas."

Throughout his generally undistinguished career, Parsons had dreamed of someday, somehow winning his sport's most significant race.

Now it suddenly dawned on Benny: "I'm going to win the Daytona 500!"

"There aren't words to describe this," Parsons said later. "This is the answer to my prayers."

A. J. Foyt won the pole at Daytona in 1976 at 185.943 mph. But then NASCAR inspectors found a bottle of nitrous oxide, concentrated oxygen that could be used to give his engine a boost of horsepower, in his car. Suddenly A. J. was no longer sitting on the pole.

Next the inspectors took a look at the car belonging to Dave Marcis, the second fastest qualifier. They discovered an illegal movable flap inside Marcis's grille that directed air away from the nose of the car and improved the aerodynamics. Marcis's time was also disallowed.

Then the inspectors turned to the third fastest qualifier, Darrell Waltrip, and discovered Darrell had been using nitrous oxide, too. That was how an Iowa bean farmer named Ramo Stott came to sit on the pole at the 1976 Daytona 500.

"If you don't cheat, you look like an idiot," Waltrip later explained. "If you do it and don't get caught, you look like a hero. If you do it and get caught, you look like a dope. Put me in the category where I belong."

A fire broke out under Bobby Wawak's dashboard on the fourth lap of the 1977 Daytona 500. "It was like sitting in front of a blowtorch," he later explained.

Somehow Wawak unfastened his safety belts and scrambled out of the blazing Chevy even before help arrived or the car had come to a complete stop. Then Wawak, who was seriously burned, sprinted off by himself in the direction of the infield care center.

Derrike Cope's best sport was baseball. He was a catcher who only turned to racing after he tore up his knee in a collision at home plate. In 1990, Dale Earnhardt led 155 of 200 laps at the Daytona 500, but it was Cope—who had never before won a big-league race in his life—who claimed the checkered flag when Earnhardt ran over a piece of metal and cut a tire on the last lap.

Gary Nelson had long been regarded as one of stock car racing's cleverest crew chiefs when NASCAR named him top cop and chief technical inspector in 1991. Asked why he placed

Nelson in such a critical, powerful position, Bill France Jr. replied, "When some of the big bankers got tired of being robbed in the 1930s, didn't they hire [bank robber] Willie Sutton as a consultant?"

Ernie Irvan, unlikely winner of the 1991 Daytona 500, was known to some as "Swervin' Irvan" because of his daring—some said dangerous—driving style.

"I like that name," Irvan said. "It beats 'Bonehead', which they named me one time."

Irvan, who left California in a pickup truck in 1982 with $300 in his pocket, worked his way up from the bottom in NASCAR. At one point, Dale Earnhardt, who had been there and done that and therefore understood what Irvan was going through, gave Ernie $3,000 to help him get by. Ironically, with five laps to go in 1991, it was Dale Earnhardt whom Irvan passed to grab the lead en route to victory at Daytona.

Richard Petty (1973-74), Cale Yarborough (1983-84) and Sterling Marlin (1994-95) are the only drivers to win back-to-back 500s. Buddy Baker was the fastest 500 winner at 177.602 mph in 1980. Junior Johnson was the slowest at 124.740 mph in 1960. Bobby Allison (1988) was the oldest Daytona 500 winner at 50 years, two months and 11 days. Jeff Gordon (1997) was the youngest at 25 years, six months and 12 days.

Dodge's return to Daytona and Winston Cup racing in 2001 got off to a spectacular start when Bill Elliott—the former master of the superspeedways who hadn't won a Winston Cup race anywhere since 1994 and hadn't won NASCAR's showpiece event since 1987—grabbed the pole. The fact that Elliott's speed of 183.565 mph made him the slowest Daytona 500 pole sitter since A. J. Foyt and his 1971 Mercury didn't bother Dodge a bit. It was Elliott's first pole anywhere since 1997. NASCAR made it an all-Dodge front row in 2001 by disqualifying Jerry Nadeau's Chevy Monte Carlo because Nadeau's roof was a half-inch too low. That put Stacy Compton's Dodge up front alongside Elliott.

Michael Waltrip waited 16 years to get to Victory Lane on the Winston Cup circuit. When he finally made it in 2001—in NASCAR's biggest race, the Daytona 500—what by rights should have been one of the happiest moments of his life was overshadowed by the death of his team owner and benefactor, Dale Earnhardt.

"I never gave up," said Waltrip after he had snapped his personal 462-race losing streak. "You can't win if you give up. I don't care how many O-fers I had.

"That 462 was just a number to me. It didn't matter at all. I've always been a good driver. The other drivers never made fun of me because they always knew I could outrun them.

"I didn't care what people wrote, what people who didn't know me thought about me. When I got this ride [with Dale Earnhardt Inc.] I said, 'All the pressure is off.' The pressure was getting an opportunity like this. I always knew I could win. I just needed the opportunity."

The 462-race drought was the longest any Winston Cup driver had ever endured before a victory. And Waltrip's victory, after starting the race in the 19th position, marked the lowest starting position of a Daytona 500 winner since Bobby Allison won from the 33rd spot in 1978. It was also only the ninth time in the forty-three-year history of the race that a driver had won from a starting position outside the top 10.

Ward Burton's 2002 victory—although he led only the final five laps of the race—was the first for Dodge in the Daytona 500 since Richard Petty prevailed in 1974. It was also only the fourth victory of Burton's Winston Cup career.

"A lot of what happens here is luck," admitted Burton after the biggest victory of his nine-year career. "We were just fortunate to be in the right place at the right time and be able to capitalize on it."

Burton became principal beneficiary when Sterling Marlin climbed out of his car during a red-flag stop to try to repair a damaged right front fender that was pressing against one of his tires.

"I had a lot of tears in my eyes," Burton confessed. "I had to take an extra victory lap to get my composure down. I can't think of anything more special than this. Nothing I can experience can ever top this."

The Dodge that Ward Burton drove to victory at Daytona in 2002 was the same one he wrecked during the 2001 Daytona 500. The car also finished fourth at Daytona in the Pepsi 400 in July of 2001 and later crashed again that year in the restrictor plate race at Talladega.

"This [car] has been a work in progress," crew chief Tommy Baldwin said. "It just likes to run real well."

Jeff Gordon saw possible victory snatched from his grasp in 2002 when he collided trying to block Sterling Marlin on a restart with six laps to go, then was ordered to the end of the line for returning to the pits for fresh tires before pit road was officially opened.

"I went from the back to the front and the front to the back," Gordon noted. "Crazy race."

"I feel like somebody went out with my wife and I just found out about it," Gordon's crew chief, Robbie Loomis observed.

In the wake of the accident-marred 2001 Daytona 500, worried NASCAR drivers wanted the superspeedway rules changed in the worst way. In 2002, many may have thought they had gotten their wish.

In an effort to reduce the aerodynamic drag on the cars and allow them to race more freely through the straightaways, and hopefully to prevent the pile-ups that had occurred at Daytona the previous year, NASCAR reduced the width (from 59 inches to 57) and angle (from 70 degrees to 55) of the rear spoilers; removed the one-inch flange from the top of the spoilers; and removed the metal air deflectors on the front of the car roofs.

"Last year [2001] it was like playing bingo," admitted Jeff Gordon. "If your number was up when the checkered flag fell, you won the race. It was all the luck of the draw. What we did last year had nothing to do with me or the car or the race team. It all came down to whether or not you were in a position to win and got lucky at the end of the race."

In plain English, NASCAR tried to put the outcome of the 2002 Daytona 500 back in the hands of the drivers. Frightened by two high-speed crashes the year before, including the accident that claimed Dale Earnhardt's life, NASCAR was seeking to reduce speeds and make the racing safer with its new regulations. The result, however, was just the opposite. More blocking and bumping led to more spinouts and pile-ups.

No one sounded happy about the early accidents during the 2002 Daytona 500—pile-ups that most people perceived to be products of NASCAR's new aerodynamic specifications for its restrictor plate races at Daytona and Talladega.

"It was a battle of wrecks," declared defending Daytona 500 champion Michael Waltrip, who finished fifth in 2002. Jeff Burton called it "a wreckfest." Johnny Benson swore he had his eyes closed because he couldn't bear to watch. "My head's still spinning," admitted rookie Shawna Robinson.

"It's probably the worst rules package we've had yet," chimed in Todd Bodine. "There is no give and take. You can't let off the throttle. It was brutal."

"The cars are going so slow—it feels like you're running 60 miles an hour out there," offered Ricky Rudd. "So everybody feels like a hero and takes a lot of chances."

"The one downfall of this restrictor plate package is that you have to block," said Kevin Harvick, who was knocked out of the race in a collision with Jeff Gordon that ignited an 18-car melee. "If you don't, you'll get hung out to dry. Then you have to go to the back and start all over again."

"Last year four or five guys raised all kinds of hell so they changed the rules," noted Bobby Hamilton, one of the drivers who was knocked out in that 18-car crash. "Now everybody is scared to death to let off the gas. And four of the guys who raised all the hell last year end up leading the race. I guess they helped themselves and nobody else."

| *Bibliography* |

Bongard, Tim, and Bill Coulter (1997) *The Cars of The King.* Sports Publishing L.L.C.

Golenbock, Peter (1998, 2001) *The Last Lap.* Hungry Minds, Inc.

Higgins, Tom (1999) *NASCAR Greatest Races.* HarperEntertainment.

Hinton, Ed (2001) *Daytona.* Warner Books.

Miller, G. Wayne (2002) *Men And Speed.* PublicAffairs.

Oakland Press, Daytona Beach News-Journal, Atlanta Journal-Constitution, various articles.

Poole, David (2002) *Race with Destiny.* Albion Press.

Zeller, Bob (2002) *Daytona 500, An Official History.* David Bull Publishing.